A Guide to
Renewing
Your
School

A Guide to
Renewing
Your
School

Lessons from the League of Professional Schools

Lew Allen
Dale Rogers
Frances Hensley
Maude Glanton
Martha Livingston

Foreword by Carl D. Glickman

Jossey-Bass Publishers • San Francisco

Jossey-Bass books and products are available through most bookstores. To contact Jossey-Bass directly, call (888) 378-2537, fax to (800) 605-2665, or visit our website at www.josseybass.com.

Substantial discounts on bulk quantities of Jossey-Bass books are available to corporations, professional associations, and other organizations. For details and discount information, contact the special sales department at Jossey-Bass.

Manufactured in the United States of America.

5\16\00

Library of Congress Cataloging-in-Publication Data

A guide to renewing your school : lessons from the League of Professional Schools/Lew Allen, . . . [et al.]; foreword by Carl D. Glickman.—1st ed.
   p.   cm.—(The Jossey-Bass education series)
  Includes bibliographical references.
  ISBN 0-7879-4691-5 (acid-free paper)
  1. School improvement programs—United States. 2. Educational change—United States. 3. Action research in education—United States. I. Allen, Lew, 1947–   II. Series.
  LB2822.82.G85   1999
  371.2—dc21
                                               98-58138

PB Printing   10 9 8 7 6 5 4 3 2 1   FIRST EDITION

The Jossey-Bass Education Series

Contents

List of Exhibits

Foreword

A Guide to Renewing Your School: Lessons from the League of Professional Schools should be a great source to all who believe the work of professional educators is "to complete, not compete with democracy" (Gutmann, 1987). All public schools (and private schools with a public purpose) have a single mission. That mission is to provide for all students an education that will accord them life, liberty, and the pursuit of happiness (Glickman, 1998).

The goal of each public school is to ensure that students become both valued and valuable citizens of an ever-questioning and ever-improving democratic society. All other school goals—academic, intellectual, social, aesthetic, economic, vocational, and recreational—are subgoals to the main one. And each subgoal is accomplished most fully through a curriculum that involves students as active participants and contributors to their own learning (see Newman and Wehlage, 1995). Thus democracy is both a means of critical study, action research, and governance among faculty, staff, students, parents, district, and community members and an end in demonstrating that all students—regardless of economic or cultural status, religious or racial identity, gender or ideology—can take their rightful place as equal, free, and contributing citizens.

The authors of this book write about work with schools that take democratic purpose seriously. Lessons are drawn from the hundred member schools involved in a long-term school renewal network called the League of Professional Schools. They share concrete and practical examples on how caring people in schools can go about the constant task of educational improvement. Examples are drawn from a range of K–12 schools serving different and diverse school populations. Through discussion of the barriers and opportunities of school-wide change, it is demonstrated that education is mostly a human rather than a technical endeavor. Change involves controversies, conflicts, frustrations, and ultimately satisfaction when educators exert a collective will to do more for all their students.

These examples should be viewed as part of a much larger school reform movement, a movement of educational optimism in the United States. This movement is composed of other kinship networks of schools, as well as individual schools and districts in rural, urban, and suburban areas that share the belief that the best education grows out of the wisdom, care, and diligence of members in local schools and local communities who take on greater authority, autonomy, and public responsibility for their students. This is the core of professional work.

In the past, the evolving work of the League of Professional Schools has been identified mostly with my thoughts and writing (Glickman, 1993, 1998). Although I am most proud to have been a major part of this work, such identification is inaccurate. The practical linkages among education, democracy, local initiative, and serious, purposeful action belong to many. The foundation of American democracy has always centered on the ideals of citizens participating in the dissemination of knowledge, informing each other, and pursuing greater truths through education to create a better democracy. At times these ideas have been mostly theoretical, without congruent practice. But many individuals and groups have pushed the definition to mean the inclusion of all citizens—not some. The struggle is to create a society governed by people, not kings or aristocrats, and to make education, democracy, and public life integral to each other.

What my colleagues and coauthors Lew Allen, Dale Rogers, Frances Hensley, Maude Glanton, and Martha Livingston have done in this book is further the school renewal agenda in explaining the practices that support its core ideas. This book is a guide and companion—not a prescription—to all those education leaders (principals, teachers, staff, parents, community members, and district and union personnel) who are committed to the promise of education and a fully functioning democracy. As a country, we certainly aren't there yet, but as these authors relate, we can learn about what is possible.

CARL D. GLICKMAN
University Professor of Social Foundations of Education
Chair, Program for School Improvement
The University of Georgia, Athens

Introduction

Teaching is an exhilaratingly complex, demanding undertaking that requires those who would master its complexities to constantly seek new insights and understandings of their practice. This book shares the lessons learned by school practitioners as they seek to provide their students with powerful educational experiences through democratic, school-wide collaborations focused on instructional and curricular renewal. Our intent is to provide practical, detailed information about how to do this work. We have included specific steps to take, activities to organize the efforts, and protocols to follow to help school-based educators and their communities transform their schools into more democratic, student-centered learning communities.

For the past eight years, teachers, principals, students, support staff, paraprofessionals, parents, central office administrators, university colleagues, and the staff of The University of Georgia's League of Professional Schools have been working together to help schools put in place a three-part framework for school improvement. *A Guide to Renewing Your School: Lessons from the League* seeks to capture and share what has been learned in this effort.

The framework that guides the work of League schools consists of a covenant of teaching and learning that is brought to life using shared governance and action research. A *covenant of teaching and learning* is a set of belief statements that captures what people associated with a school want students to know and be able to do, the type of instructional practices they believe will bring about these desired results, and a description of how students will demonstrate mastery of the desired skills and understandings. *Shared governance* is a democratic process that gives all a school's stakeholders the opportunity to actively participate in bringing their covenant to life. *Action research* is an information-producing process that provides feedback and guidance as a school works to carry out the terms of its covenant.

This framework was created in the real world of schools and described by Carl Glickman in his book *Renewing America's Schools: A Guide for School-Based Action.* In 1983, Glickman, a professor in the College of Education at The University of Georgia, began working with a veteran principal of a small rural high school who was frustrated in his attempts to implement changes that would benefit students. The resulting efforts led to documented success in using the framework for democratic, school-wide renewal to drastically reduce the school's drop-out rate and increase student achievement as measured by standardized tests, and these results created interest from other schools. Shortly thereafter, a large urban elementary school used the framework to reduce its retention rate of minority students and increase teachers' confidence in their professional abilities, while a primary school—in its first year of implementing the framework—significantly improved its climate. Given these encouraging results, Glickman sought to form collaborations with a wider variety of schools from across the state of Georgia.

Overview of the Book

All schools are unique, and what works in one won't work in exactly the same way in another. The goal of this book is therefore to provide enough detail to be helpful without being overly prescriptive. We expect that our suggestions will be adapted to fit varying contexts. We also intend that this book will serve as an ongoing companion to those working with and in schools rather than as a one-time read.

Chapter One clarifies the purposes of the League's framework and provides a general overview of the issues and a definition of each part of the framework. Readers of Glickman's book, *Renewing America's Schools: A Guide to School-Based Action*, will note that he described the three parts of the framework as consisting of a *covenant, charter,* and *critical study process.* These terms are interchangeable with the ones used in this book: *covenant of teaching and learning, shared governance,* and *action research,* respectively. The chapter then goes on to provide guidelines for what a school can do to lay a foundation for implementing the League's framework. The main thrust is to help the reader see the need for a school's faculty to clarify their beliefs about teaching and learning and school renewal so that they can make an informed decision about whether they want to do the kind of work necessary to implement the framework.

The following chapters offer recommendations on how to implement each of the three sides of the framework: a covenant of teaching and learning (Chapter Two), shared governance (Chapter Three), and action research (Chapter Four). These chapters include stories of success, cautionary tales, general suggestions, step-by-step actions to take, and forms to be used. Each chapter also includes a self-monitoring guide (developed by the League's Demonstration of Practice Initiative, a group composed of practitioners from League schools that have made significant progress in implementing the framework) to assist schools in charting their progress. The guides identify traits that indicate high implementation for each part of the framework, and trace the progression a school would go through before fully implementing the relevant aspects of the framework.

Chapter Five deals with issues that cut across working with the three sides of the framework, including change, finding time for teachers to work outside their classrooms, team building, getting outside facilitation, and building internal capacity. It concludes with a brief summary of recent research into the issues of school-wide change—and specifically what League schools have accomplished and learned in the process—and some recommendations for action.

At the end of the book, a Resources section lists publications that provide additional information on action research and assessment, shared governance and collaboration, democratic education and school reform, and the League itself.

Looking Ahead

It is possible for a school to adopt the League framework on its own, but doing the work is easier with the support and advice of others engaged in the process. Two professional organizations among many, the National Staff Development Council and the Association for Supervision and Curriculum Development, provide conference opportunities as well as useful and practical publications. In addition, with the Internet, e-mail listservs, and chat rooms, direct interaction with other practitioners around the country and around the world is truly only a moment away. But the most valuable resource, as has been stated by League schools for years, is the opportunity to network with each other. Network with other educators whenever you can, and make the time at meetings just to find out how other schools are going about this work and to learn about new or innovative practices. The more familiar you become with the accomplishments of schools employing the League framework, the more exciting and the less intimidating the prospect will be!

Acknowledgments

As you read this book, it will become apparent that we, the authors, are indebted to the work of Carl Glickman, founder of the Program for School Improvement and the League of Professional Schools. Carl brought us each into this exciting work, and continues in the role of adviser, friend, and colleague.

We are also indebted to Emily Calhoun, who directed the League during its first year and who remains a valued colleague and source of information and ideas. Her work in the field of action research is internationally known, and she continues to offer her special expertise to the League and its schools.

Barbara Lunsford followed as director. Under Barbara's guidance, the League doubled in membership, and when after six years Barbara left the League to return to the principalship, our membership exceeded one hundred schools. As the leader of a League school, Barbara continues to provide us with practical suggestions about how the implementation of the League's framework plays out in the real world of schools and to jog our memories through her extensive knowledge of the League and its schools.

Throughout the history of the League, groups of League educators have added to our work and understanding. We particularly want to thank the Action Research Consortium, the League Information Network Consortium, and the Demonstration of Practice Initiative.

We are also grateful to our colleagues on the League staff: Teresa Edwards, Glory Griffin, and Ann Seagraves, and to our graduate students who over the years have contributed so much to our efforts.

Our many colleagues in the College of Education at The University of Georgia continue to add depth to our work.

We could not carry on this work without the support of the College of Education, the BellSouth Foundation, the Lettie Pate Evans Foundation, the Pittulloch Foundation, Annenberg Rural Challenge, and the UPS Foundation. We are grateful for their support and their belief in the League.

Finally, heartfelt appreciation to the teachers, principals, support staff, parents, students, community members, and central office personnel of League schools, past and present, for providing us with the lessons that we share here. Their unflagging devotion to their schools and to the promise of American education continues to inspire and inform our work.

The League of Professional Schools

Carl Glickman founded the League of Professional Schools in 1990. Membership in the League was made available to all Georgia public schools, K–12. Twenty-two schools joined in the League's first year. Within three years, membership tripled. Currently there are over a hundred diverse elementary, middle, and high schools in the Georgia League, with affiliated networks in Nevada and Washington. There are large, small, urban, suburban, and rural schools in the League. Some schools serve predominantly middle- and upper-middle-income families, while some serve very poor families. Some have racially mixed populations, and others have a majority of one cultural or ethnic population. The one thing that all these schools have in common is their belief in the power of democratic principles, as realized through the League's three-part framework, to guide successful, ongoing school renewal.

The purpose of the League is to provide its member schools with support as they implement the framework. The League Congress, a governing body made up of representatives from each school, originally set forth the services the League provides to its schools. The congress believed that the key source of expertise that needs to be tapped to facilitate this work is found in the schools and their communities. While League meetings often involve educators from outside the League, the main function of all meetings is to provide League practitioners and their stakeholders with opportunities to learn from each other. League consortia, task forces, on-site visits, summer institutes, and a newsletter also provide school people with opportunities to learn from each other as we deepen our collective understanding of our work. For additional information about League services, see Chapter Five. Contact information for the League is as follows:

League of Professional Schools
124 Aderhold Hall
The University of Georgia
Athens, GA 30602
Phone: (706) 542–2516
Fax: (706) 542–2502
E-mail: lps@coe.uga.edu
Web site: www.coe.uga.edu/lps

The Authors

The authors, who are codirectors of the League, all spent many years working in schools before coming to the League.

Lew Allen has been a member of the League staff since its inception in 1990. Prior to that, he served as a secondary special education teacher and a university instructor. Lew holds an Ed.D. in educational administration from The University of Georgia.

Dale Rogers has been a middle school language arts teacher, an assistant in the Georgia Facilitator's office of the U.S. Department of Education's National Diffusion Network (NDN), and coordinator of a project to develop assessment programs for school support personnel (for example, media specialists, counselors). She joined the League staff in 1996. Dale has an Ed.D. in supervision from The University of Georgia.

Frances Hensley has also been affiliated with the League since its inception. She has taught at the elementary and middle school levels and has served as Georgia State Facilitator for the NDN. Frances has an Ed.D. in adult education from The University of Georgia.

Maude Glanton was a teacher, district office coordinator, reading supervisor, and principal of a League school before retiring and joining the League's staff part-time in 1997. Maude has an Ed.S. from Georgia State University in reading.

Martha Livingston also joined the League staff in 1997 as a part-time codirector. She has been a secondary school teacher, a curriculum director, and a superintendent, and she is currently professor of educational administration at Valdosta State University. Martha earned an Ed.D. in educational leadership from the University of Alabama.

As codirectors, we plan League meetings focused on deepening our understanding and that of our school-based colleagues about the complexities of implementing the League's three-part framework for school-wide renewal. At these meetings, we attend and conduct breakout sessions focused on the work of the League. We also provide a diverse selection of sessions to help schools make informed decisions about their curricular, instructional, or organizational initiatives.

We help create consortia to study and facilitate specific areas of League work and serve with League school practitioners on them. We plan and participate in summer institutes that focus on problem areas identified by the schools. Along with university colleagues and practitioners from League schools, we spend many days in League schools conducting on-site visits focused on each school's self-assessment of its progress in implementing the League's framework. We then follow up with summaries of our observations that we send back to the schools for their use. We analyze all on-site summaries, looking for patterns in school actions and for common concerns and best practices, then use this data to guide future services.

We also benefit from the work of colleagues at The University of Georgia who conduct research with League schools and share their findings through conversations, presentations, and writings. Finally, we solicit the people who work in League schools to capture and share the lessons they have learned through case studies, manuals, and essays. The content of this book is grounded in and reflective of all of these experiences, collaborations, and writings.

A Guide to
Renewing
Your
School

Chapter One

Understanding the Framework for School Renewal

Making the commitment to implement the framework is a big step for a school. This isn't tinkering. It is agreeing to make basic changes in the way a school does business and to open up classroom procedures, activities, and assessments to collective reflection. Roles for teachers, students, administrators, parents, support staff, and community members will change, and people will be asked to act in different ways. Procedures, both formal and informal, will be revamped. A school community that quickly and easily decides to implement the framework most likely is ill-informed about the effort required.

People don't make substantive changes quickly and easily. Consequently, it is important that a school take the necessary time to decide whether this approach to school renewal aligns with the way that the people in and associated with the school think about how the school should improve its work with students. In this chapter, we provide a brief overview of the guiding framework of the League of Professional Schools and answer questions about laying the foundation for the framework. We then use Chapters Two, Three, and Four to give you specific details about each part of the framework and how they work together to create a democratic learning community.

Why Is the Framework Necessary?

The three-part framework was created to address the question of how a school can set goals based on genuine consensus, take collective action, and study the effects on student learning. Schools implementing the framework will enhance the educational experiences of students by using democratic principles to focus on instructional and curricular issues. We stress this because we have found that if schools aren't careful, they get caught up in changing school structures and processes and lose sight of the bottom line: improved student learning. Implementation of the framework must have an impact on classrooms and how teachers teach, students learn, and parents participate in their children's learning.

There are multiple reasons why students benefit when their schools implement this framework:

- *The central purpose of public schooling in America has always been to educate its future citizens in how to participate in and maintain a democracy* (Glickman, 1998). By modeling a belief in the power of democracy, both in its governance and in its classroom procedures and activities, schools provide students with real-life lessons in what it means to be a participating citizen in the United States. As Glickman states:

  Empirical evidence suggests that when democracy is practiced as a way of learning and living in schools, it leads to astonishing success in the intellectual achievement of all students, from preschool through adulthood, and creates citizens who can lead satisfying and valuable lives. . . . Until we understand that democracy is the best way to learn and to make individual and collective choices—and until we put that understanding into practice in our classrooms, schools, and communities—then the word democracy will continue to be merely a rhetorical device that obscures our true lack of belief in and commitment to it. [1998, p. 4]

- *Public schools have an obligation to meet the needs of all students—not just those from mainstream, politically connected families.* When schools become democratic places for all stakeholders, they can better address issues of value conflicts, gender, race, religion, and multicultural perspective.

- *Teaching is an extraordinarily complex task that is never completely mastered, so students benefit when schools are learning places for everyone.* Teachers, administrators, support staff, parents, and community members all need to continue learning. If teaching were a simple, minimally challenging profession to master, then schools would not need to find ways for people to work together to constantly learn about and get better at what they do. But it isn't. In summarizing the research on what helps schools provide their students with the best possible instruction, Mike Schmoker (1996) writes, "Evidence for the benefits of collaboration, rightly conducted, are overwhelming" (p. 12).

What Is the Framework?

As shown in Exhibit 1.1, the framework consists of a covenant of teaching and learning that is brought to life through shared governance and action research. The three parts are all essential to making the framework function.

Covenant of Teaching and Learning

A covenant of teaching and learning captures the beliefs that people in a school and its community hold about what they want their students to know and be able to do, what teaching and learning practices will bring about these competencies, and how students will demonstrate the acquisition of these competencies. "It becomes the screen for [examining instructional practices and] saying 'Yes, we do that here' or 'No, we will not do that here'" (Glickman, 1993, p. 24). Each of a school's instructional and curricular goals, objectives, and activities is filtered through the question, Is this within the letter and spirit of our covenant?

"A school may immediately find that certain practices (teaching methods, materials, allocation of instructional time, grouping of students, grading and evaluation practices over the normal course of a day) are consistent with the covenant, while others simply are not" (Glickman, 1993, p. 27). Without a covenant to help define and clarify a school's beliefs and practices, the collective energy of the individuals in the school is often fragmented or focused on the immediate issues of the day rather than on what all would agree, in their more reflective moments, should be done to achieve the long-term goals of the school community.

Shared Governance

Under shared governance, schools reach a common understanding of how decisions are to be made in bringing to life the beliefs stated in their covenant. A shared governance process "spells out who is to be responsible for what, the composition of decision-making bodies, the decisions to be made, and the process to be used" (Glickman, 1993, p. 29).

Shared governance ensures that the decision-making process is democratic and accessible to all. Clearly written guidelines that lay out how decisions are to be made help ensure that everyone in the school knows the rules, and that processes and procedures will not change for expediency or on the whims of a few.

Action Research

Action research helps a school identify, clarify, and plan actions that are meant to bring to life the beliefs articulated in its covenant. Then, once decisions are made, action research provides feedback as to the effects the decisions are having. This creates an ongoing cycle of study, plan, act.

A school's ability to bring about school-wide renewal that benefits students is closely tied to its capacity to study and reflect on how its practices are affecting all students. Action research helps schools stay focused on student goals. While action research can be used to document whether programs, new initiatives, or new structures have been put in place, its more important and vital role is the study of what is happening to students as a result of the changes that have been made.

Integrating the Framework

An example of how the three parts of the framework are tied together can be found in the work of one school that has dedicated itself to implementing League principles. This school's covenant expresses the belief

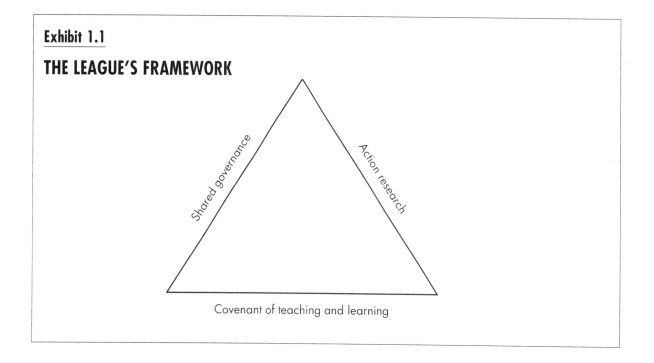

Exhibit 1.1

THE LEAGUE'S FRAMEWORK

Shared governance

Action research

Covenant of teaching and learning

that learning is enhanced when students are active participants in their own education. Because this is a part of the school's covenant, everyone associated with the school (including the students) is aware that this is one of the main beliefs that drives the school's instructional and curricular efforts. Given this school-wide belief, the decision-making process outlined in the school's shared governance by-laws focuses on making students active participants in their own learning, in addition to addressing the other points in the covenant. The school's staff development program, teacher evaluation process, assessment practices, teacher and student recognition arrangements, parent night programs, and peer coaching efforts all reflect this belief and the other beliefs found in the covenant.

When a new teacher suggests that the governance process be used to devise a better way to load students onto the buses at the end of the day, the reply is that the governance process is only used to bring the school's covenant to life and not to cope with the myriad of other issues that arise from time to time.

The school's action research is focused on understanding how its efforts in promoting active learning are affecting students and teachers. Individually and collectively, teachers study their efforts in actively involving their students in their own learning, as well as working with students to devise ways for them to demonstrate their learning. The shared governance leadership team makes sure that all that is being learned is also being shared school-wide.

Unlike many schools that have individuals and various groups pulling in many different directions, this school is a focused community of learners working together to constantly improve the educational experiences of its students.

How Do We Decide Whether to Proceed?

Typically, a school and its community have a core of individuals who are generally excited about and ready to work for change. And there are people who tend to be distrustful of most proposed changes. It is a good idea to begin by setting up a committee or task force including people who come from all points on this continuum and who reflect the school's population as to gender, race, teaching experience, and teaching assignments. Such a heterogeneous committee will increase the chances that people will feel their opinions are represented on this group. Keep in mind, this group is not being chosen as the school's new governance team, but rather to help the people in the school and community think about their beliefs about shared governance, action research, and ongoing reflections about teaching and learning. There will be time to choose a shared governance leadership team later, when and if a school decides to implement the framework.

How Do We Begin to Define Our Beliefs?

The committee mentioned in the preceding section should provide the leadership in this effort. When people enter into discussions about the framework without first reflecting on its underlying assumptions about teaching and schooling, they often find it difficult to understand the varying positions that people take. Unexamined—or at least unarticulated—beliefs about the implications of implementing the framework can leave people pulling in different directions without understanding why.

People who think teaching is a relatively simple profession that can be mastered within the first few years will not see the need for their school to create a structure that creates an ongoing conversation about teaching and learning. They will resent the time spent in discussions because they feel they already know what needs to be done and how to do it. They will see time spent reflecting on teaching as wasted.

People who see student failure as a simple issue that needs action, not reflection and study, will not see the need for schools to have covenants of teaching and learning, nor will they see any reason to conduct action research on instructional issues. These educators may believe that student failure is tied to the motivation of the student, the decline of society, or the neglect of parental responsibilities. Such educators tend to have confidence in their beliefs about what needs to be done. It will take time to have some faculty look to themselves rather than outside themselves. But it's the first step in revealing the philosophical stance of the school community.

These are the types of issues and questions that people connected to a school generally don't talk about in formal settings. Normally, teachers and administrators are not asked to go on record about their beliefs. Discussions of the type described here get differences out on the table where they can be considered, providing people with opportunities to examine beliefs that they may not have examined before. Without exploring these issues, the framework can't be thoughtfully considered.

The following procedures will help people think through and express their own beliefs, learn about the beliefs of others, and get a feel for what the faculty as a whole thinks about schooling in general and the League's approach to school renewal in particular.

Suggested Activity

The organizing committee assigns teachers, parents, students, and community members to small groups (around six people per group). Each group selects a monitor and a spokesperson. The monitor's job is to ensure that everyone in the group participates. The spokesperson's job is to take notes and to share the essence of the group's discussions.

The organizing committee then selects questions from the list in Exhibit 1.2 that they believe will spark the most productive discussions. (Alternatively, they could write their own questions.) It is important that the small-group facilitators ensure that everyone in the group participates in these discussions. This will minimize the behind-the-scenes discussions that can undermine this process. All doubts, concerns, and questions need to be expressed so they can be dealt with during the conversations.

Once the small groups have met and each person in the group has spoken to the topic, the whole group then convenes. At this meeting, the recorders for each group share their notes (on flip charts, trans-

---

Exhibit 1.2

SUGGESTED QUESTIONS FOR SMALL-GROUP DISCUSSIONS

1. How are curricular and instructional decisions currently being made in our school? What are the strengths and weaknesses of this process?

2. What is happening in our school that increases development of our thinking about instructional improvement?

3. What do we have happening in our school that hinders development of our thinking about instructional improvement?

4. Do you believe our students would benefit if we all worked closely together to identify instructional strategies that would improve, expand, or fine-tune our current instructional practices?

5. What are your thoughts about the power of democratic principles to guide school governance and instruction?

6. What information do we currently use to tell us how we are doing in providing students with the best possible educational experiences?

parencies, or other widely visible media) and summarize what has been said in the group.

There are several alternatives to simply having recorders summarize each group's discussion. One is to have all the group representatives sit in a circle with an empty chair as part of the circle. Representatives share and discuss what was said in their groups while the rest of the faculty listens. If any faculty or staff member wants to be a part of the conversation, they come forward and sit in the empty chair. After they have had the opportunity to make their point, they return to the audience and others wanting to enter into the discussion can come forward and take their turn in the empty chair.

After the meeting, the notes recorded on the flip chart sheets for each group can be placed on the walls in the teachers' workroom so people can further examine what their colleagues are thinking and feeling. This list of concerns, suggestions, thoughts, and feelings can provide those leading the effort with important information about the degree of alignment between the beliefs of their colleagues and implementation of the League's framework.

This should be the beginning of an ongoing dialogue rather than a one-time experience. It is important that enough time be devoted to this so that everyone has multiple opportunities for open and honest discussions about their beliefs.

Taking Stock

At this point, everyone in the school will have had an opportunity to discuss the beliefs underlying the framework. As mentioned earlier, some people will hold beliefs that support the school's moving forward to make a commitment to implementing the framework. Others will be skeptical. They may hold beliefs that don't match this type of school-wide activity, or they may believe that teachers will be manipulated into thinking they are going to share in decisions when, in reality, important decisions will continue to be made by the same people who have always made them.

There may be some who have gained the principal's ear and fear that this new way of doing business will result in their losing the influence that they currently have. Some veteran faculty members have seen many new innovations come and go and have good reasons to assume this is just another fad and not worth getting excited about. These beliefs and concerns need to be aired, discussed, and in some cases addressed. Even then, many long-held beliefs will not be overcome easily or quickly.

It may be helpful and necessary to get some outside facilitation in this effort. Some schools may need a skillful facilitator to help people express themselves and work through their concerns without creating animosity and division. It is very important that people's feelings and opinions be respected, and—most important—listened to. An outside facilitator can help make sure this happens.

Even with the best of efforts, most schools will not have everyone excited about considering implementing the framework. But bridges shouldn't be burned at this point. If the organizing committee believes a majority of the people are favorable or at least open to learning more (the committee may need to poll people informally or formally), the school should move on to the study of the framework, working hard to keep lines of communication open through a continuing dialogue. However, if a majority of the people have strong misgivings about even considering a school-wide effort to focus on teaching and learning, then more time needs to be spent exploring their concerns. If the principal is not in favor of exploring the framework, then there is no reason to press on. A school can't implement this framework until the principal is willing to support it 100 percent.

Looking Ahead

After a school has studied the beliefs behind the framework and the framework itself (Chapters Two, Three, and Four), it is ready to decide whether to make a school-wide commitment to implement the framework. How does a school know if it has the necessary support to move forward? Schools wanting to be a part of the League are required to have an 80 percent vote, on a secret ballot, in favor of implementing the framework. The rationale behind this is that until a school has a critical mass of people who support the process, the framework will not be truly implemented. People will go through the motions if they are required to, but the spirit, motivation, and ownership of the process won't be there to sustain the effort. Some schools have been able to go through the complete process outlined here in a few months and receive the 80 percent vote. Other schools have taken considerably longer to gain the school-wide understanding and commitment needed to get started.

Please consider this cautionary note when your school community votes favorably: just because at least 80 percent of the people in your school voted to implement the framework, that doesn't mean that there is no longer a need to continue to study its possibilities. Gaining school-wide acceptance and ownership of a covenant of teaching and learning, building a deep understanding of the implications that democratic practices hold for both school governance and classroom instruction, and learning how to study the impact that initiatives are having on students are ongoing processes that will continue to need the best thinking of all a school's stakeholders.

What Are the Stages in Implementing the Framework?

Keep three qualifications in mind as you review the stages outlined here. First, this work is never complete; implementing the framework is an ongoing process that does not play out in a linear fashion. A school will make progress in one area and take a step back in another. Or, because of personnel change or some other factor outside its own control, it will lose much of what it has gained and have to go back and start over. Second, schools vary widely in their experiences with the framework—including how long it takes to put the framework in place. And finally, the progression included here is based on our experiences with the first group of schools that joined the League in 1990. All these schools started from scratch, in that the idea of sharing the governance and conducting action research based on a school-wide covenant of learning was completely new to them. Schools joining the League now are generally more informed about this type of work and, in many cases, already have parts of the framework in place.

A helpful way to think about the stages that schools go through as they implement the framework is to consider a distinction that Carl Glickman (1993) made in *Renewing America's Schools*. He identified three kinds of schools: conventional, congenial, and collegial. In *conventional* schools there is an expectation of autonomy and people work in isolation. Teachers go to their rooms, close their doors, and teach in privacy. In *congenial* schools, people work in isolation as they do in conventional schools, but the school in general has a more social atmosphere. In these schools people often socialize both inside and outside of school. Meetings are pleasant and relaxed and differences of opinions are avoided or smoothed over. *Collegial* schools differ from both conventional and congenial schools in several ways.

> *Collegial schools are characterized by purposeful, adult-level interactions focused on the teaching and learning of students. Peo-*

ple do not necessarily socialize with one another, but they respect their differences of opinion about education. Mutual professional respect comes from the belief that everyone has the students' interest in mind. The result of such respect is seen in school meetings, where the school community members debate, disagree, and argue before educational decisions are made. Even in the hottest of debates, people's professional respect for others supersedes personal discomfort. People believe that differences will be resolved and that students will benefit. Social satisfaction is a by-product of professional engagement and resolution, of seeing how students benefit, and the personal regard in which adults hold one another. . . . Being collegial means being willing to move beyond the social facade of communication, to discuss conflicting ideas and issues with candor, sensitivity, and respect. [Glickman, 1993, p. 22]

Given this conceptual background, the following stages are offered as a general guide as to what happens as League schools use the three-part framework to become more collegial places.

Stage One: Beginning

- A shared governance process is in place—but it is not written down. People's understanding of how shared governance is eventually going to interact with action research and the covenant is vague, at best. People know they are working on creating a shared governance process but they have different understandings as to why.

- It is not clear in people's minds which decisions will continue to be made by administrators and which decisions will be made through shared governance. The decision-making process is not explicit in this area and people, including administrators, are confused.

- People believe that decisions can be made democratically by simply replacing the administrators as chief decision makers with a team of teachers and administrators. Consequently, the decision-making process is more democratic than it was, but not as democratic as it's going to be.

- There is a high degree of skepticism about whether this will result in real change or whether it is just going to be another passing fad. Some people wonder if "they" (the district or school administration) are really going to let teachers take an active part in the life of the school. Others are concerned that a group of teachers will come into power and lord it over the rest of the faculty. Principals are worried that teachers don't have a grasp of the big picture and may make decisions that have unintended negative consequences.

- The people who are elected or appointed to leadership positions are mostly the same people who are already in leadership positions (that is, grade level managers, lead teachers, department heads) or who hold informal clout (the teachers who always seem to be in the forefront with all new initiatives, those with long tenure, those who have the principal's ear). The people serving on leadership teams are generally restricted to the certified staff, and teams don't reflect the makeup of the population of the school and its community.

- Despite the uncertainty, those who take an active part in the initial activities surrounding the work are excited about the possibilities. They see this as a very positive direction for the school to take.

- Action research activities are limited to general needs-assessment surveys that are not directly related to the school's covenant of teaching and learning. This is sensible because at this point the school doesn't have a covenant of teaching and learning. It has a mission statement that is not used in any practical sense.

- Only a few people understand how the three parts of the framework will eventually fit together to create a school-wide process for school renewal.

- During this stage, most people don't have strong feelings about the effort, because in their opinion, not much of substance has happened. Many are taking a wait-and-see stance.

Stage Two: Developing

- By-laws have been written to guide shared governance. Only a few people know them very well.

- Fewer people are simply being appointed to leadership positions, and more democratic ways of identifying leaders are being explored.

- Leadership team members realize they must stay in closer communication with those they represent. The lines between leaders and the rest of the school community are beginning to blur as people start to realize that being a leader is more about making sure everyone is involved and less about making decisions for others.

- Most of the issues that the leadership team addresses are focused on creating better working conditions for teachers.

- Most of the information gathered is focused on areas that are peripheral to instruction (things like noise in the cafeteria, or handling tardiness).

- Shared governance procedures are clarified to define more clearly what decisions are to be made democratically and what decisions are to be left to the administration.

- The school has a covenant of teaching and learning that consists of broad statements about student outcomes and the purpose of the school in general. Most people have only a vague notion of what's in the covenant and how it is to be used.

- All in all, some people are getting very excited about what the school is beginning to accomplish. Others are still taking a wait-and-see attitude, but as they see for themselves how the framework functions, they begin asking questions and take more interest.

Stage Three: Emerging

- The shared governance process reflects people's understanding that it is important for all members of the school and its community to be active participants in this effort. Parents, paraprofessionals, and students are now included on leadership teams and are taking part in the process.

- Many people understand that the purpose of shared governance is to ensure that everyone's best thinking is being brought to bear on teaching and learning issues. Shared governance is understood as being more about helping people work together on improving their teaching and less about political rules and regulations that everyone must follow.

- The school's covenant is revised to focus more on teaching and learning. Leadership teams are beginning to focus most of their time on bringing the covenant to life. Students, parents, and teachers are aware of the covenant and understand that it can serve as a guide to their actions.

- Action research efforts reflect a growing interest in teaching and learning issues. Information is being gathered about how students are being affected by the school's efforts.

- Leadership teams are working hard to improve communication so that everyone understands how to get items on the agenda for team meetings, minutes of meetings are distributed to everyone, and meetings are opened to everyone. Leadership teams establish task forces made up of people not on the leadership team to study issues and take the lead in initiatives.

- As people talk with each other, understanding across grades and departments begins to build. People begin to trust that they all have the best interest of the students in mind.

- A majority of the people in the school understand the three parts of the framework and how they fit together to increase the school's capacity to serve students.

- Most important, teachers, students, parents, and administrators are all focusing their efforts on constantly improving the teaching and learning process, and students are beginning to benefit.

Stage Four: Working

- Most people understand the power of the framework and many of the activities involved in its implementation are institutionalized.

- People see results for kids. Action research is being used to inform the decision-making process, and it is possible to document positive effects for students. The covenant is known to most people in the school, including students, parents, and community members, and it guides the work of the school.

- Leadership team members are rotating off to make room for others to take their turns. Some of the skeptics are serving on leadership teams and now believe that this is for real.

- Principals see themselves as facilitators of the decision-making process. They have a clear understanding of what decisions are to be made democratically, what decisions are to be made by the principal with input from others, and what decisions are the principal's alone.

- People feel a part of the school and realize they can never go back to having no voice in the life of the school.

- The school provides professional development to help the new people who arrive each year understand what the effort is all about and take part in it.

Summary

Schools rarely manage to implement deep and lasting improvements in student learning as a result of undirected good intentions. The three parts of the League framework give a school a structure that allows it to democratically define for itself what good teaching and learning looks like (covenant of teaching and learning), the rules all agree to follow to bring the covenant to life in classrooms (shared governance), and how it will know if it is making progress and what adjustments need to be made (action research).

Early discussions about the framework and how faculty and staff are implementing it in their own school are essential in the decision-making process. The stages presented in this chapter are part of the information process; a school community should know that schools vary in the amount of time it takes to put the framework in place and that schools do not move smoothly from one stage to the next. It is much messier than that. Schools at any given time will have elements of their work that could be characterized as being in Stage Four while other elements are in Stage Three and some are in Stage One. The main factors that affect the implementation are how hard and how smart people will work. The administration must work hard to understand the framework and embrace the beliefs that drive it, and the school must spend the necessary time and resources to help people work together to bring about the implementation.

It is also important to understand that getting the framework in place is only the beginning. Once the framework is in place and the school's capacity to make wise decisions for students is adequate, the work of continuous school renewal begins.

Chapter Two

Creating a Covenant for Teaching and Learning

For our schools to become genuinely good institutions, they must be undergirded by a strong set of beliefs about teaching and learning. A covenant is a document that sets forth these beliefs about teaching and learning as guiding principles. It unifies and guides instructional focus and is the foundation of successful League schools.

Although many education professionals express their beliefs about teaching and learning with great passion as individuals, it is imperative that school communities as collective bodies clarify and record their beliefs about teaching and learning. According to Glickman (1993), the covenant is more than a vision of teaching and learning—it represents a sacred obligation to live in accordance with what it contains. The covenant should be developed by the whole school community through a democratic process. It should focus on teaching and learning and what that looks like in a school, and it should guide future decisions (Glickman, 1993).

School renewal efforts must be guided by a set of agreed-upon beliefs about teaching and learning that provides for the best interest of all the students we serve. In Glickman's work, as in some League schools, the covenant embodies the purposes of education in a democratic society (Glickman, 1998). The beliefs endorsed in a given covenant, however, are those unique to a particular school community. It is the school community that develops and sanctions a set of principles to guide its own purposeful engagement, and in so doing, equips the school with a strong and lasting document.

What Should a Covenant of Teaching and Learning Cover?

As we noted earlier, a covenant of teaching and learning captures the beliefs that people in a school and its community hold about what they want their students to know and be able to do, what teaching and learning practices will bring about these competencies, and how students will demonstrate the acquisition of these competencies. Let's take a closer look at this definition.

Most schools already have mission statements, which correspond to the first part of a covenant: a statement of what they want their students to know and to be able to do. The problem with stopping here is that such a statement doesn't provide enough information to guide people's actions or to let anyone determine whether the school is making progress in carrying out its mission. For example, say one part of a school's mission statement challenges the school to create lifelong learners. What, then, should the teachers, administrators, students, parents, and community members do to create lifelong learners? How will they know which students are, in fact, becoming lifelong learners—and which ones are not? The covenant will need to include more information about teaching and learning.

First, the school community needs to state what types of instruction or educational experiences they believe will result in lifelong learning. Such statements will need to be specific enough that they are observable. For example, people may believe that instruction that requires students to be active in their own learning, connects the subject to the community and the real world, and engages students in in-depth analysis of subjects is more likely to develop lifelong learners than passive, teacher-centered instruction.

Finally, the people in this school will identify how students will demonstrate the skills and knowledge tied to the beliefs about lifelong learning. Identifying how students are to demonstrate lifelong-learner competencies does not mean compiling the dozens of assessments that the students will encounter over the course of their schooling. Rather, it refers to categories or types of assessment such as public demonstrations, portfolios, or certain scores on sections of standardized achievement tests. These categories are then applied to specific areas of instruction. For example, with regard to the ability to "connect the subject to the community," a demonstration might involve requiring the student to identify a community problem, plan a way to address the problem, and then use skills from across several subject areas to explain how to carry out the project. Without this understanding of how learning is to be demonstrated there is no way for the school community to know what works and what doesn't or if they are making progress in realizing the vision they have for what they want their students to know and do.

How Do We Begin?

This is a long process and one often fraught with conflict. Before beginning, consider the time involved and plan the general steps to be taken. Specific strategies should be put in place so that all constituencies have a voice. The League's *Orientation and Planning Workbook* (1997) includes these general guidelines:

1. Engage faculty in conversations about the League's definition of a covenant.

2. Develop strategies for receiving input from the school's community—that is, teachers, support staff, students, parents, community members, business partners.

3. Form a representative group to review input and draft the covenant.

4. Gain democratic endorsement of the covenant from all stakeholders.

5. Announce and publicize completion of the covenant.

The covenant forms the base of the framework and is developed through a process that involves all constituents and is implemented through the shared governance process. Therefore, the shared governance by-laws or charter (see Chapter Three) should probably be in place before the covenant-development process is too far advanced. Implementing the framework is not a linear process, however, and people need to be thinking about their underlying beliefs and their ability to participate in shared governance at the same time, as each will inform and enrich the other. In general, the covenant development process will involve the work of various small groups such as task forces, ad hoc committees, or liaison groups. It should be clear to whom these groups report (for example, to the faculty, to the school improvement team), how their work will be disseminated, and how final decisions will be made. Therefore, an operational shared governance process could expedite the development of the covenant.

No matter which groups participate in covenant development or the role each may play, it should be clear whether each group's input is advisory or voting (if a vote is proposed) on the final covenant. It is possible to consult some constituencies such as business partners while keeping the final decision within a smaller set of constituencies. Keeping things up-front will help eliminate future problems. Tacit understandings and unwritten rules do little to help solve disputes or to move the covenant development process forward.

How Do We Get the Whole School Community Involved?

To begin this work, consider holding initial discussions among the school community somewhere other than at the school. This tends to give weight to the importance of the conversations; it's not just another faculty meeting. Possible off-campus meeting sites include a local resort or retreat site; a private home; a meeting room at a public library, church, hotel, or bank; a state or local park recreation center; or a conference room or boardroom in the offices of an educational partner. To kick off the meeting, create a conference atmosphere with refreshments or a continental breakfast and a suitable souvenir. A packet of materials containing articles about developing a philosophy or how to articulate beliefs, a personalized notebook, or a tote bag with the school's logo—or several such items—will do a great deal to help set the tone of the meeting. Providing the participants with the type of materials and ambience one encounters at a professional conference underscores the importance of the work they are about to undertake.

Once the logistics have been nailed down, the discussions could begin with a variety of activities that would help the group think about and articulate what they believe about teaching and learning. The exercises in Exhibit 2.1 are based on the premise that people's beliefs about teaching and learning determine what their practice will look like. Belief statements of the type specified in these exercises describe specific concepts about education (for instance, more students learn by doing than by listening); they don't describe hoped-for outcomes (we want our students to be lifelong learners) or convey philosophical points of view (schools are caring places for all students). When we clarify our beliefs, they can guide us as we make our school experiences relevant and meaningful.

It's not realistic to think that a school community could develop a covenant during a two-day retreat. These first meetings and conversations are just the beginning of the discourse in which the school community will

Exhibit 2.1

ACTIVITIES FOR CLARIFYING BELIEFS

The Writing on the Wall

This exercise is for small groups.

Departments or grade levels meet, discuss, and list their beliefs about teaching and learning on sheets of chart paper. Lists from all departments or grade levels are placed on the walls in the teachers' lounge, workroom, or other highly frequented location to foster thought and discussion prior to more formalized work.

This exercise is useful for all small groups whether at PTA meetings or meetings of the full school community. The list generated can be displayed in the office or school foyer.

Interview

This exercise is a good way of breaking up a larger group. It requires a facilitator to move the group along, to bring the group back together, and to lead the final discussion. The exercise is done in pairs.

1. During department or grade-level meetings, for example, group members pair off with one as interviewer and the other as the respondent.

2. The interviewer asks the respondent to spend three to five minutes stating important principles of teaching. The interviewer only listens and can only ask questions for clarification.

3. The partners reverse roles for another three to five minutes.

4. Each partner moves to another person, and the interviews are conducted following the same procedures. This process continues for a specified period of time.

5. The group reassembles and comes to consensus on the beliefs, which are to be presented to the school community.

My Most Memorable . . .

For teachers, parents, community, students. Small- to moderate-sized groups.

This activity is an excellent way to get school faculties and the larger school community engaged in discussions about what makes good teaching and learning.

Participants engage in a discussion of such topics as "My Most Memorable Learning Experience," "My Most Memorable Teacher," or "My Vision of a Perfect School."

Students respond in their classrooms to writing prompts such as: "Our school would be an even better school if... " or "If I were the principal I would... " Younger children can dictate responses to the teacher or draw pictures to illustrate their ideas. The teacher compiles the ideas of the students and presents them to a subcommittee or task force appointed to put together ideas from across the student body. Compiled student responses are

Exhibit 2.1 (continued)

highlighted during morning announcements or in some other way, showing students that what they contributed is valued and will become part of the conversation as the school community develops the covenant.

Beliefs About Teaching and Learning

The introduction to participants should emphasize the point that a covenant of teaching and learning undergirds the education program and guides instructional practices on a daily basis, and explain that this exercise is designed to evoke clear statements of belief that can be compiled into a covenant uniquely appropriate to the school that constructs it. Participants will complete the sentence stems in small groups, then discuss in small groups and present to the larger group. A facilitator should be appointed to move the groups along, to bring the groups back together, and to compile final statements for distribution.

1. Participants in each group write as many belief statements as the group can agree upon, completing the following sentence stems (using additional sheets of paper if needed):

   Students learn best when _____

   Good teaching involves _____

2. Each group then compiles its statements on the chart paper provided.

3. The groups select spokespersons to post their charts and present their statements to the larger group.

4. The facilitator collects all the statement sets and compiles them for distribution and review. The document may be further refined or used to begin subsequent discussions.

Develop a Theme (an example from a League elementary school)

A League school conducted this exercise as a way to engage the school community in conversations on a particular theme, which led to the development of the covenant.

The principal and a group of staff members and parents met during the summer to decide on an acronym as a way to launch the new year with a theme.

At the beginning of school a mysterious acronym FOHGYCB was posted throughout the building and painted on the floor of the entrance foyer. During preplanning, staff members were engaged in conversations to solve the acronym. Figuring out what the letters stood for was the springboard to serious subsequent faculty, staff, and student discussions of what they believed a great school to be. Once the acronym was solved, students took flyers home that asked parents to think about how the school could ensure that all students at the school would Find Out How Great You Can Be (FOHGYCB).

become engaged. Often discussions will continue over the year at numerous meetings involving different constituencies. Action research data is also often necessary to focus ideas and opinions more clearly. Throughout this process, the school continues to function with all the usual requirements and constraints on time and energy that daily schooling demands. Therefore, all participants should understand when beginning this development process that refining and honing the educational beliefs of so many will take time, but that the length of time to completion should not diminish their enthusiasm or the importance of the task.

The Reasons for Universal Engagement

Everyone for whom the school is important must work together through a democratic process to develop and agree upon a set of guiding principles about teaching and learning. We are reminded of the need for inclusion when we compare a covenant with Conant's definition of democracy as "a small hard core of common agreement surrounded by a kind variety of individual differences" (Conant, 1953).

The school leader must serve as the flag bearer in this effort by sincerely encouraging all members of the school family to speak out, to make their beliefs and ideas about teaching and learning known. All stakeholders must know that their input is valued, that no particular person will hold sway over what goes into the covenant. When everyone is heard in the development of the covenant, they are energized to exert greater effort in bringing the covenant to life. This is yet another reason why it is imperative that all members of the school family are involved.

If any member of the school family remains silent, others may take that silence as consent—an assumption that might be far from the truth. The effort to ensure that no one voice dominates underscores the essential nature of the covenant as a democratically derived document in which everyone has a stake and in which all are invited to participate.

League educators generally agree with these affirmations regarding school-wide participation in the covenant development process. Unfortunately, a reality check reveals that getting everyone involved is often a Herculean task.

Techniques for Building Collegiality

Before beginning the discussion of beliefs, you may wish to engage in some team-building activity that will heighten the level of acceptance and trust among the group. Teachers in particular are not always accustomed to talking about what they actually believe. This experience can also provide an opportunity for staff to get acquainted on an informal level. This kind of activity can build a sense of collegiality that is essential to school renewal.

Students must also be engaged in this process through meaningful dialogue. Their thoughts must be acted upon so that they will see that their beliefs and opinions are valued. Through strategic questioning and discussion, teachers can move students beyond their usual focus on improving the food in the cafeteria and abolishing homework to their often unarticulated ideas about what they want from the school experience. Even kindergarten students are able to present insightful ideas about what teaching and learning should look like. They must actively participate in the process—and they must see positive implementation outcomes that result from their ideas and input. Exhibit 2.2 describes some techniques for engaging students in the process.

Parent participation is harder to achieve. Parents often don't know what they can do to be of value to the school. Where parent participation in the school is slight, the first step is to increase that involvement by making the parents feel that they can make a contribution. Inviting parents to

---

Exhibit 2.2

ACTIVITIES INVOLVING STUDENTS

From a League School Survey

Members of a school's governing council met to discuss the value of a covenant. The members of the council created a student survey to obtain their ideas first. The principal also spoke to the student council members (second through fifth graders) about the process and importance of writing a covenant. The survey was given to the students in all grade levels. Children in primary grades generated their ideas together with the assistance of the classroom teacher. The responses were reviewed and the exact words and phrases of the students were recorded.

The Committee for School Improvement also responded to the survey items and added its input. In cross-grade groups as well as other groups, teachers responded to the children's issues and statements. They were careful not to lose the voice of the children as ideas were organized and revised. The children's ideas are included in the covenant.

Developing a School Creed

The development of a school-wide creed is another excellent way to hear what students believe about teaching and learning. Have each class engage in a discussion and come up with three statements that they think should be in the school creed. Have the student council synthesize all the responses into the creed. Then distribute a copy to all classes.

come in as mentors, speakers, or once-a-week instructors indicates that they are valuable to the school. Leighninger and Niedergang (1995) suggest that the school hold mini-workshops on parents' night to answer the parents' concerns about their children. Workshops could include tips on helping a child learn to read, an explanation of high school graduation requirements, factors in selecting a college, coping with the adolescent years, effective discipline. Once parents feel a part of the school and trust that they are valued, then conversations can begin on the covenant. Exhibit 2.3 provides an example of one such process.

Soliciting input can take many forms and regardless of the avenues explored provides some fundamental data about the school's instructional and curricular programs. The point to remember whether in gathering data or seeking input is to keep activities, information-gathering tools, discussions, and meetings focused on teaching and learning. A parent survey beginning with a broad question (say, What do you think the school needs to do to be better?) may generate responses that include very specific suggestions about individual teachers or the way the building is maintained or designed, criticisms of a particular curriculum, or advice about the football schedule. All valuable input—but none of it is what you need to know in developing the covenant. Keep the questions focused on specific ideas, skills, and principles related to teaching and learning processes. A school can use a variety of techniques and activities like the ones sketched in Exhibit 2.4 to solicit the input of students, parents, and other constituencies.

Once you have all the input you've sought, the covenant committee or development team can filter through responses for those that specifically address teaching and learning. The ideas and thoughts generated could be collated and presented in various ways to constituencies for further input.

Exhibit 2.3

PARENTS IN ACTION

The principal, the School Improvement Council chairperson, and a group of parents met to plan strategies that would increase the number of parents who would come and share their beliefs about what makes a great school. A committee of parents designed attention-getting flyers to encourage other parents to come to an interactive session to share their beliefs about teaching and learning. The flyers were sent home by students and as well as through the mail. Prizes were given to classes with the highest parent attendance at the "WHAT'S YOUR IDEA" meeting. Parents brainstormed ideas for a better school.

Such discussions help form specific principles and beliefs from general statements. Your process may differ from that of other schools, but it is generally one of draft and revise.

How Do We Focus the Covenant on Teaching and Learning?

Covenants should contain statements of what students are expected to know and be able to do, what teaching and learning practices will bring about these competencies, and how students will demonstrate the acquisition of these competencies. How learning is demonstrated refers to the decision about how students are to demonstrate what they have learned at the end of specific stages of schooling (say, at the end of first grade, or upon middle school graduation). For example, the covenant can specify that students will publicly demonstrate knowledge through recitations or

---

Exhibit 2.4

TIPS FOR ENGAGING PARENTS, STUDENTS, AND COMMUNITY MEMBERS

- Have students interview their parents, grandparents, and neighbors for their ideas.

- Send home a survey developed by a task force of the school improvement team.

- Have a committee of parents develop a survey for distribution at PTA meetings and other gatherings.

- Invite teachers, parents, community members, and volunteers to focus group sessions aimed at mastering the techniques of group engagement in discussing ideas about teaching and learning. Participants then become group facilitators for other meetings.

- Have draft copies of the statement of beliefs posted on the walls of the main entrance of the school with space for additional input. After a specified period of time, the sheets are collected and revisions made. One school posted these at a local grocery store.

- Use the school newsletter as a vehicle for presenting the belief statements for review by parents. The modifications and revisions are recorded on the newsletters and returned to the school.

- Invite constituents to leave their statements of beliefs on the school voice mail system or respond by e-mail.

performances, produce a series of interdisciplinary, exploratory projects, or complete a series of portfolios over a high school career.

It is imperative that schools remain focused on teaching and learning and resist the temptation to include well-intentioned statements about other areas of schooling. One method of critiquing your covenant is to ask about each statement, Is this statement about teaching and learning? and Can the ideas expressed in this statement be demonstrated? The answers will determine if the statement is appropriate for a covenant. This isn't always easy. But asking such questions will help distinguish between fads, innovations, initiatives, and specific curriculum.

A statement, for instance, that refers to the idea that all children can learn is indicative of a vision statement, mission statement, or other document that reflects the philosophy of the school. The covenant begins with a mission statement, but it goes beyond that; its content is more action-oriented. A covenant statement may refer to the idea that students learn best through hands-on learning or that learning is an active process. Such statements can actually be visualized; one can picture students conducting a science experiment, building a replica of the Globe Theater, painting murals, planting a garden, and so forth. However, this belief statement makes no reference to a particular program. It does not say, for instance, that students learn best by using Reading Recovery, the Mechanical Universe, or another specific curriculum or activity. These may indeed be used to bring a particular covenant statement to life, but the statement itself refers to a particular concept about teaching and learning that is applicable regardless of the innovation or program currently in place. So the covenant statement is more specific than a vision statement but broad enough to include a variety of activities, programs, units, or curricula.

It is also imperative that the people in a school go through the process of writing their own covenant of teaching and learning. The examples in Exhibits 2.5 and 2.6 are intended to help communicate what a concise covenant might look like, not to provide schools with a ready-made document. Following the process of writing a covenant is a very powerful experience, and simply adopting another school's covenant, no matter how plausible and appropriate it may appear, will shortchange the school community and leave it without the deep learning and bedrock agreement needed to move forward with effective implementation of the framework.

Please note the qualities found in both sample covenants. Each includes a realistic, doable vision of what successful students should know and be able to do. They both list specific beliefs about teaching and learning that are observable and directly related to the vision. And they state

Exhibit 2.5

SAMPLE COVENANT OF TEACHING AND LEARNING

Mission Statement

At Smith School we will actively engage all students as a community of learners so that they become problem solvers, effective communicators, good citizens, and lifelong learners.

We believe that our mission will be realized if

- Students are actively engaged in their own learning.

- Students' learning is linked to real-world experiences.

- Students' learning is monitored and assessed using authentic, ongoing assessment techniques.

- Students engage in a mixture of individual and cooperative activities.

- Students are challenged to use information from across subjects to construct their own knowledge in solving complex problems.

- Students are given opportunities to make responsible decisions about their learning and the governance of their school, and are held accountable for their actions within and outside the school.

Student Demonstrations

Smith School students will demonstrate their abilities as problem solvers, effective communicators, good citizens, and lifelong learners through a variety of products, presentations, and projects. These demonstrations will range in scope from those that reflect complex, multi-discipline, multi-year learning done in a community setting, both within our school community and the community at large, to more specialized, single-discipline learning that is demonstrated within classrooms. Some demonstrations will be reviewed by panels of teachers, peers, parents, and community members, others by individual students and their teachers.

Exhibit 2.6

SAMPLE STUDENT COVENANT

Wilson Elementary School's Student Covenant of Teaching and Learning

We, the students at Wilson Elementary School, will work among ourselves and with our teachers and parents to make sure we all know how to:

1. Express our feelings and thoughts to others.
2. Make wise choices about what we want and need to learn.
3. Make what we're learning helpful to our classroom, school, home, and community.

To help us do these things we will:

1. Have good attendance and be on time.
2. Try different ways to learn.
3. Decide with our teachers and parents what we need to know.
4. Decide with our teachers and parents if we are learning what we need to know.
5. Share our learning with others.

We will show ourselves and others that we know how to express our feelings and thoughts to others by being good teammates with other students; taking part in classroom meetings; showing other students respect and kindness; asking our teachers, parents, and classmates appropriate questions that help us with our learning.

We will show ourselves and others that we know how to make choices about what we want and need to learn by keeping a diary of our best work and explaining to our class-mates, teachers, and parents why what we are learning is important. We will show ourselves and others that we can make what we're learning helpful to our classrooms, school, home, and community by doing projects that make things in those places better.

how the school will know if students are demonstrating the desired qualities stated in the vision statement.

How Do We Celebrate Completing Our Covenant?

The completion of the covenant should be a school-wide event engendering feelings of accomplishment and reflection. "We all somehow knew that the covenant that we endorsed that day would become well-worn paths tomorrow," commented a teacher in a League school. A covenant is the product of vision and hard work. It will ensure that students benefit from the collective thinking and action of the entire school community. Completing it is, therefore, reason for celebration. In fact, when visiting League schools, we hear many positive comments about the various ways that they have publicized their covenants. We often hear comments like these:

> *This process injected new energy and enthusiasm in our vision for our school. In unveiling our covenant we dedicated ourselves anew to our agreement upon beliefs about teaching and learning.*

> *The process of developing our covenant has been a great plus for our school family. This experience helped build the self-confidence of staff. We were all excited about the opportunity to determine the destiny of our school.*

Some ideas for marking the completion of the covenant with school staff and community are to display a large parchment copy in the front hallway and include the text in the school handbook. If there's a core statement, you can have it stenciled on T-shirts, posters, bookmarks, and book covers. For more detailed publicity, run an exclusive issue of the school newsletter dedicated to the covenant, write an article about the process for your district or local newsletter, and place copies with local storekeepers and business partners. Particularly for students, it's also useful to hold a pep rally or assembly.

The dialogue within a school community during the development of the covenant builds the needed foundation for bringing the covenant to life. After its completion comes the time to begin the day-to-day work of bringing the collective vision to life.

How Do We Move from Beliefs to Action?

"Conviction is worthless unless it is converted to conduct" (Carlyle, 1965). So it is that the final audit for a covenant is conducted through action research of daily practices within the school to monitor and evaluate how well the covenant is coming to life. Covenants contain principles of teaching and learning, and the goal for schools is to eliminate the gap between the words on the parchment and actual practice in the school and classrooms. As the total school staff becomes more directly involved in bringing the covenant to life in its daily practice, a variety of ideas will be developed, decisions made, and risks taken.

Shared governance, of course, is the process by which the covenant is actualized. When a school community looks to its covenant, discussions and decisions will occur based on the covenant statements. A covenant statement will generate a variety of engrossing questions:

How do we ensure the kind of education we have defined?

Do we institute mastery learning?

Do we alter our schedule for more instructional time?

Should we move to an integrated curriculum or a disciplined-based arts program?

Do we replace remedial programs for a learning styles–based instructional program?

Do we eliminate tracking?

How do we implement this practice?

Should we teach all students using the techniques of gifted education?

How do we assess students?

Exhibit 2.7

ACTIVITY TO PUBLICIZE THE COVENANT, FROM A LEAGUE HIGH SCHOOL

Covenant conversations conducted by members of the school family led to the contest to develop a logo based on the school's covenant. It was felt that this strategy would bond and unify the school around its agreed-upon beliefs. The logo contest began with a morning announcement that generated much enthusiasm for the idea. Students participated, a winner was declared, the logo was adopted, printed, and posted throughout the building. As a result, the entire student body was familiar with the school's covenant.

How do we involve parents in this activity?

What will be the role of the student?

What kinds of staff development will we need?

Are study groups a way to prepare us for the new program or curriculum?

Will we run a pilot program?

What kinds of action research will we need to study the results of these decisions?

These questions focus the decisions on classroom instruction, which is the most important function of the covenant. What each school values should be reflected in its classroom activities and the kinds of student assignments it encourages, the materials it purchases, and the awards it gives, the assessments it uses, the staff development it offers, and the language it uses, as well as in the organization of the school day and the allocation of school funds, and in numerous other ways and areas. The covenant serves as a touchstone for the values underlying all these decisions, so it should be displayed so as to be accessible to the full school community. Efforts should be made to ensure that the covenant is a living document, not just an ideal.

For example, one statement in the covenant in Exhibit 2.5 asserts, "Students are actively engaged in their own learning." What implications may this have for the decisions to be made? What kinds of programs, activities, equipment, schedules, instruction, linkages to other agencies, or resources would need to be looked at to implement a program in which students would truly become active in their own learning? Should the school develop a new schedule allowing free time for students to conduct experiments on their own, to develop multimedia programs, to publish their own newspaper, to engage in service learning, or to undertake joint projects with local governmental agencies? Should instruction become more facilitative and less prescriptive? What projects should students be allowed to explore freely? These are the issues the shared governance body, task forces, and liaison groups will need to explore and to gather information about.

We have stressed throughout this chapter that developing covenant statements is an extremely thoughtful process. Each belief arrived at has enormous implications for the way the school is structured, the way students and teachers interact, the expectations for students, and so on. To bring the covenant to life will result in looking at what is and what needs to be—and that in itself will take a lot of work.

To determine if the covenant is genuinely reflected in the day-to-day work of the school, the following monitoring activities were developed by the Demonstration of Practice Task Force, a group set up by the League to determine what practices one might encounter in a high implementing League school:

- Shadow students to see how the spirit of the covenant is or isn't affecting their learning.

- Administer surveys to various stakeholders for their input about how the covenant is being lived in the school.

- Audit meeting agendas to see if issues dealing with the covenant are being discussed.

- Invite on-site facilitators and other outside colleagues to look for signs of the covenant in people's actions.

- Encourage teachers to keep journals and reflect on their efforts at incorporating the spirit of the covenant in their classrooms.

- Using action research, study student work for reflections of the covenant's implementation.

A school community works hard in developing a covenant and wants to see it manifested in the day-to-day life of the school. Monitoring will keep the faculty, staff, students, and community diligent about bringing the covenant to life. Exhibit 2.8 provides a useful guideline for determining what has been accomplished and in planning what is left to be done. In the exhibit, schools just starting out will see themselves mainly in the "Emerging" column; those who have defined their work more thoroughly will be in the "Focusing" column; and those schools that understand the work and have implemented this aspect of the framework will be in the "Expanding" column.

Review Questions

The following questions will help refine the process of developing a covenant:

1. How would a covenant guide our work with students?
   - What can we do that would make this a useful, living document?
   - How will a covenant keep us focused on instruction?

- What role does a covenant play in relation to the charter and the action research processes?

2. What type of statements would we include in a covenant?

- Would these be specific or general types of statements?

- How would the statements found in a covenant differ from those in a mission statement?

- What are sentiments that we would want to avoid in writing a covenant?

Summary

The covenant guides the work of the school, for it is how the whole community views teaching and learning and how the results of these beliefs are translated into student achievement. Through the covenant, a school community defines for itself what goals it wants to achieve, determines how it is to implement those goals through the decisions it makes, and studies whether it has achieved those goals through action research. The covenant should be displayed; it should be accessible to the full school community. Efforts should be made to ensure that the covenant is a living document, not just an ideal—it is the core of the work of the school.

Exhibit 2.8

SELF-MONITORING GUIDE: THE COVENANT

		LEVEL OF IMPLEMENTATION				
		1	2	3	4	5
TRAIT	**Component**	**Emerging**		**Focusing**		**Expanding**
Trait 1: The covenant is developed, revisited, implemented, and monitored, following democratic, inclusive procedures.	Development	Small, nonrepresentative group or individuals write the draft of the covenant.		A small group representative of the school community writes the draft of the covenant.		All stakeholders (teachers, students, parents, community members, and business partners) have the opportunity to share in writing the covenant.
	Approval and Reflection	The covenant is approved by the staff with little reflection.		The covenant is approved, with some opportunities for reflection by the full school staff.		The full school community approves the covenant, with opportunities for reflection.
	Revisiting	Once written, the covenant is not revisited.		The covenant is revisited irregularly.		The covenant is revisited regularly.
Trait 2: The covenant is focused on teaching and learning.	Belief Statements	Statements are not only about teaching and learning but also about values, goals and results, the purpose of the school, expected roles of different groups and individuals, and the climate of the school.		Most, but not all, statements deal with beliefs about teaching and learning.		All statements are focused exclusively on beliefs about teaching and learning.
	Action Statements	Many of the statements are general in nature and call for actions that cannot be observed, measured, or demonstrated.		Most statements call for actions that can be observed, measured, or demonstrated.		All statements call for actions that can be observed, measured, or demonstrated.

Exhibit 2.8 (continued)

TRAIT	Component	LEVEL OF IMPLEMENTATION				
		1 **2** Emerging		**3** Focusing	**4**	**5** Expanding
Trait 3: The covenant is widely known, understood, and used to guide the actions of all stakeholders.	Understanding	Few people understand what is in the covenant or use it to guide their actions.		Most people understand the covenant, but only a few use it to guide their actions.		Nearly all understand the covenant and use it to guide their actions.
	Alignment	Decisions made through shared governance are not aligned to covenant belief statements.		Decisions made through shared governance are occasionally aligned to covenant belief statements.		Decisions made through shared governance are consistently aligned to covenant belief statements.
Trait 4: The covenant's implementation is monitored.	Monitoring	Very little is known about whether the covenant is used to guide people's actions.		There are few ongoing procedures for monitoring whether the covenant is being used to guide people's actions.		Multiple ongoing procedures are used to monitor the covenant's implementation from various points of view: students, teachers, parents, community members, business partners, and other stakeholders.

Source: Demonstration of Practice Initiative (1997–98).

Chapter Three

Designing a Charter for Shared Governance

Shared governance is the decision-making process through which the school's covenant is brought to life, providing the leadership for conducting action research. Shared governance is a collaborative process that ensures all persons democratic involvement in decisions about teaching and learning.

Often it is the premise of shared governance that first attracts a school community to the League's school renewal process. Principals see participation with school colleagues in decision making as an avenue for creating a broad base of support for school programs, and teachers first see shared governance as the opportunity for their involvement in the school's instructional and curricular decisions. The practice of shared governance includes both perspectives but is much broader when viewed as a premise of the League of Professional Schools. Shared decision making is the preferred method of leadership within schools because it involves all the stakeholders. But more important, shared leadership promises to enhance learning opportunities for students by yielding better decisions with a by-product of better achievement results (Schlechty, 1990).

Teachers involved in school decision making provide a synergy of problem solving that creates tremendous opportunity for instructional improvement. Often termed "empowerment," participation in decisions about the critical areas that directly affect their work of teaching and learning seem the most important to teachers (Short and Greer, 1997).

We have learned that real school improvement is not changing facilities or cleaning up the grounds—it's making a difference in teaching and learning (Hanson, 1997). The concept of participatory decision making in some form is a common strategy for many school improvement initiatives. Shared governance within the League's framework offers the structure to implement the beliefs and best practices espoused in the school's covenant.

What Is the Charter?

The question of how a school practices shared governance is addressed in the school's charter, the written by-laws or processes and procedures for decision making. The term *charter* as used by the League denotes the document created through and about the shared governance process and should not be confused with the use of the term in connection with charter schools. Whether a school refers to its written governance procedures as a charter or something else is not important. But Glickman (1993) uses the term in *Renewing America's Schools,* and for consistency it will be used here to denote the guidelines for how a school devises and implements shared decision making.

The charter concept is not unique to the League of Professional Schools but is used in other models of shared governance and site-based management. School charters document a set of previously unwritten understandings and make clear who is responsible for what decisions as well as how the decisions will be enforced (Sagor, 1996). In League schools, charters set forth the role of the leadership group, how decisions will be made, what decisions will be the focus of shared decision making, and what form the representative body will take. The goal is not for shared decision making to work with all decisions but to emphasize decisions that affect teaching and learning and to do so in a democratic way.

League schools have been effectively implementing plans of shared governance around three guiding rules of governance (Glickman, 1993, p. 29):

1. Everyone can be involved in decision making.

2. No one has to be involved.

3. Once decisions are made, everyone supports the implementation.

Essentially, the one-person-one-vote principle puts the power of decision making in the group as opposed to leaving it with traditional authority figures. Concentrating on instructional issues within the school's sphere of influence limits the work of the shared governance body to the critical issues of teaching and learning and enables the group to function effectively.

How Do We Begin?

A concern often voiced by new schools in the League is, How do we start developing our shared governance process? Although the League recognizes and encourages individuality and the discovery of what works best for each school, a school new to shared governance might consider engaging in a series of conversations about developing collaborative decision making along the following lines:

- What are our expectations of shared governance?

- Who should participate in shared governance?

- How will participants be selected?

- What decisions will be the focus of the shared governance plan?

- What are the roles of the participants—principal, teachers, students, others?

- Once the by-laws are established, can we amend them?

- How may the roles of administrators and teachers change? What might they stop doing? What might they start doing?

It is important, also, to look at what formal ongoing groups are currently functioning in your school. If some decisions about teaching and learning are already made by some kind of group process, use what you have as a beginning. It's not always necessary to begin from scratch.

What Kinds of Decisions Should Our School Community Consider?

The most difficult aspect of shared governance appears to be determining what issues and topics should be considered. Schools should focus on their own locus of control—that is, on issues that are within the control of the school. Emphasis should be on what we, the school, can do—as opposed to what we think others outside the school should do (Glickman, 1993).

Practically speaking, where school board policy is in effect, there is no decision to be made at the school level. Employees are to implement the decision of others when dealing with policy issues. This is not to imply that employees in individual schools should not seek changes in policy, when needed, through prescribed channels. Locus of control also implies that schools should confine efforts to their own structures, practices, or programs as opposed to concentrating on the activities of the district office or other schools within the district, even if such action would enhance the effectiveness of their school. For example, decisions for other schools, such as a high school's choosing activities for the feeder middle school, are beyond the school's locus of control (Glickman, 1993).

Teaching and learning are at the core of the school and are, therefore, the central focus of decisions. Shared governance that focuses on administrative functions tends to lose sight of improving teaching and learning. A school's focus is embodied in the covenant. As discussed in Chapter Two, the covenant is the document in which the school and community set forth what they believe about teaching and learning. The shared governance body should look to the covenant as a check to the kinds of decisions it should make.

It is useful to classify school decisions according to their relevance to teaching and learning. Based on Glickman's work (1993), Exhibit 3.1 provides a quick reference point in determining whether issues are directly focused on the covenant of teaching and learning.

Zero Impact Decisions

Decisions that primarily involve issues of adult employees are referred to as "zero impact" because they have little influence on teaching and learning. Examples of zero impact decisions are parking issues, concessions in the teacher's workroom, or playground duty. The shared governance body

---

Exhibit 3.1

FOCUS OF GOVERNANCE: EDUCATIONAL IMPACT ON STUDENT LEARNING

Zero Impact	Auxiliary Impact	Core Impact
Parking spaces	School budget	Instructional budget
Lunchroom supervision	Hiring of personnel	Staff development
Faculty lounge	Deployment of personnel	Parent involvement
Sunshine fund	Personnel evaluation	Instructional programs
Adult recreation		Student assessment
Dress code		Curriculum

Source: League of Professional Schools (1997), Glickman (1993).

should typically avoid assuming responsibilities that can be more efficiently and appropriately addressed by the school's administration.

Auxiliary Impact Decisions

Auxiliary impact decisions relate to teaching and learning—but not as directly as curricular and instructional issues. Personnel issues, for instance, are generally considered auxiliary. Schools will define what has auxiliary impact somewhat differently. Some League schools, for instance, see personnel decisions as having a direct impact on teaching and learning, particularly when staff have input into the interview and hiring process. Other faculties and staff choose not to be involved in the personnel selection process, and therefore see the impact as less direct. Room assignments, the purchase of certain computers, or parent programs may be viewed as important or secondary issues, depending on how the faculty and staff view their impact.

Core Impact Decisions

Core impact decisions are defined as those that directly affect teaching and learning. Decisions on budgets for instructional programs, personnel selection, curriculum, and staff development all relate to bringing the covenant to life. Core impact decisions are made over time, usually as a result of the school's action research and as an extension of the covenant.

Who Participates in the Shared Governance Process?

Shared governance in the local school implies the involvement of the principal, teachers, paraprofessionals, instructional support personnel, parents, business partners, community members, and, as appropriate, students. While the process should be open so that all persons have the opportunity to participate, no one should be required to do so—choosing not to take an active part is itself a form of participation. The whole community needs to accept that even with representative input in decision making, there will always be some decisions that do not please all participants. Thus a part of the shared governance process is a commitment from the participants to support and implement a decision once that decision has been collaboratively made (Glickman, 1993). No one has a veto on decisions made by the group.

While schools will always consider some decisions in large groups or total faculty, League schools have found a great deal of practicality in developing representative decision-making groups reflective of the gender, ethnic, and socioeconomic populations that make up the school and community. Among League schools, the decision-making group has a number of different names, such as School Instructional Team, School Improvement Team, or School Council. In this chapter, the representative decision-making group is called the "School Improvement Team."

Teachers should form the majority of the School Improvement Team because they have a preponderance of the expertise and responsibility for school decisions related to teaching and learning (Glickman, 1993). The reference to teachers is a general one and should be determined by individual schools, but usually refers to certified personnel who work with students in a teaching and learning capacity. The building principal should be a standing member of the group. Other members of the school's administration may be a part of the School Improvement Team as needed, or depending upon the size of the school.

Different models exist among League schools for participation on a School Improvement Team. While the elementary grade level, middle school instructional team, or high school department models of representation are most common, the use of instructional teams across grade levels, units, or secondary disciplines has proven to be effective. Some schools elect representatives from across grade levels where each grade is represented in each group or from the school as a whole. Most often, members of the School Improvement Team are elected to represent a specific constituency. For example, the second grade teachers or the paraprofessionals elect a representative. Student members may be elected by grade level or serve as representatives of the student council. Parent members are often the officers of the PTA or PTO or serve as grade parents or as mentors. Representation by business partners (some schools include them all if their number is few) or community members at large should be spelled out in the charter.

Within these basic models, the representatives may serve on task forces or liaison committees, which provide the School Improvement Team with information regarding issues that are to come to a vote. The role of the School Improvement Team members typically includes keeping the representative group informed, bringing prospective decisions to the table for consideration, and generally being as effective as possible in representing their respective groups. Exhibit 3.2 presents an organizational chart used by many League schools.

Exhibit 3.2

ORGANIZATIONAL MODEL FOR SCHOOL-WIDE INSTRUCTIONAL DECISION MAKING

School Improvement Team

Liaison Group 1

Liaison Group 2

Liaison Group 3

Liaison Group 4

Liaison Group 5

Liaison Group 6

Liaison Group 7

Task Force 1

Task Force 2

Task Force 3

What Is Included in a Charter?

The charter provides a written structure of how decisions will be made in a League school. This document is written by members of the school faculty and staff, parents, and other constituents in a process that allows input and ultimate affirmation of the entire school community. The involvement of all staff is at the heart of the development of the charter. If only the few teachers and administrators who are often associated with the power structure of the school are involved in the development or implementation of the charter, the remaining staff will lack faith in the process, and it will most certainly fail. A successful League principal notes that issuing invitations to participate will almost certainly be ineffective. Solicitation and persuasion are necessary leadership behaviors in achieving full inclusion in the process.

School charters are unique but a review of charters from a number of League schools indicates there are some similarities in components. For example, as in Exhibit 3.3, charters often begin with an overall statement of belief or commitment to the principle of shared governance. This statement serves as the introduction to the charter and references the school's vision and how shared governance functions to enable the vision.

School Improvement Team or Representative Body

Typically, the school's charter should address the School Improvement Team. This group is given a name that is appropriate for the school and reflective of its role. The number of persons who serve on the team is determined by the school's size or organization. The representational pattern is an important issue for consideration. While schools should pay close attention to see that all groups are represented, a pattern of how these groups are represented and to what degree they are represented needs to be addressed in the charter. For example, provision for administrators, teachers, paraprofessionals, parents, and others to participate is critical to the development of the charter. How much representation to give to each group is essential to the School Improvement Team's ability to function.

Decisions about membership include what group is represented, how the member is selected, the number of representatives for any one group, and the length of service. Whether representatives serve from grade level, team, or discipline groups or from the school at large is an important

Exhibit 3.3

CHARTER OF A LEAGUE PRIMARY SCHOOL

The school improvement committee is TEAM (Together Everyone Achieves More)

- To provide a means for shared decision making by faculty and staff for instructional improvement.
- To provide an opportunity for open communication among faculty, staff, and administration.

The TEAM is composed of two teacher representatives per grade level, the school counselor, media specialist, two paraprofessionals, head custodian, food service manager, secretary, bookkeeper, assistant principal, and principal. The TEAM meets on the first Thursday of each month, or as needed.

Process

1. Issues may be brought to the TEAM by any member or as a referral from the total faculty or from the suggestion box.
2. Once received, the issue may be assigned to a committee for research, input may be sought from the entire faculty, or assistance may be solicited from the central office.
3. Feedback is given to the TEAM who will determine by consensus what recommendation is made to the faculty.
4. A two-thirds majority vote is required before adopting new procedures.
5. TEAM members will be elected by their group to serve for a two-year term.

---

determination. Caution should also be taken to ensure representation of all instructional staff as well as all instructional and auxiliary personnel such as counselors, media specialists, special education support staff, janitorial and cafeteria workers, paraprofessionals, and others who have a role in the work of the school and the lives of its students.

The selection process for individual team members by their representative groups centers around election, selection, or volunteering. The charter should also provide guidance for the terms of office for the School Improvement Team representatives. The document should allow for some type of rotation so that the School Improvement Team does not have all new members at once. Schools frequently use two- or three-year terms. The sample charter in Exhibit 3.4 goes into greater detail on this matter.

Exhibit 3.4

CHARTER OF A LEAGUE ELEMENTARY SCHOOL

Introduction

We want our school to become a community of learners. We believe that school, home, and community collaborate to provide a safe, caring, and enriching environment for all learners. Our goal is to develop responsible citizens who are lifelong learners.

Our school uses the democratic process as our underlying framework from which all decisions are made. Everyone has an equal opportunity to be involved in the decision-making process. Once decisions are made, their implementation is fully supported.

Composition of Action Response Council

A.R.C. will consist of thirteen members:

Administrator (1): standing member.

Teachers (7): one per grade level.

Support Personnel (3): includes media specialist, counselor, nurse, music specialist, special education, Title I, SIA, gifted, physical education.

Instructional Assistants (1).

Staff (1): includes child nutritionists, custodians, classified personnel.

A.R.C. members will be elected by their constituency. Members will serve two-year terms. Six positions will be available for election each year. Members may NOT succeed themselves. (Exception: The initial A.R.C. membership will include 6 three-year terms and 6 two-year terms before the standard two-year rotation process begins.)

Vacancies on the team are to be filled for unexpired terms by elected staff for representative groups. Members must forfeit the remainder of their term if reassigned to a position not within the constituency they were elected to represent.

Job Descriptions

Chairperson

- Sets agenda for Council meetings.
- Schedules regular meetings with the principal for input.
- Publishes Council's agenda on Monday before the meeting.
- Conducts Council meeting: States objectives of meeting, outlines procedures for reaching decisions, facilitates communication, summarizes decisions.

Exhibit 3.4 (continued)

- Sets agenda for communication family meetings.
- Serves as the school's representative to the League of Professional Schools.

Vice Chairperson

- Assumes duties of the Chairperson in Chairperson's absence.
- Assists Chairperson in planning Council meetings.
- Assumes duties assigned by the chairperson in conducting meetings and making presentations.
- Serves as the liaison between the Council, task forces and standing committees.
- Schedules the first meeting of task forces, publishes meeting dates on school announcement sheet, helps with the selection of Task Force Chairperson and recorders if requested, provides the task force presentation to the Council.
- Files task force reports for future review.

Recorder

- Takes attendance at Council meetings.
- Records decisions reached by the Council.
- Records permanent data such as committee assignments.
- Maintains or arranges maintenance of file containing Council business.
- Keeps minutes of meetings and distributes a written summary within two days.
- Assigns someone other than chairperson or vice chairperson to take minutes when absent.

Team Leader

- Conducts meetings.
- Gathers and reports information, concerns, and ideas of the team to the Council.
- Informs communication teams of activities and decisions of the Council.
- Appoints a recorder who will take minutes that will be published and turned in to the chairperson who turns them in to the A.R.C.

The leadership of A.R.C. will consist of a chairperson and vice-chairperson elected from among the 13 members. Each will serve a one-year term. The vice-chairperson will succeed the chairperson. Nonvoting membership will consist of the assistant principal (standing) and issue-oriented delegates who appear on the meeting agenda.

Exhibit 3.4 (continued)

Procedures

A.R.C. meetings will be held the first Thursday of every month for approximately one hour. Additional meetings will be scheduled as deemed necessary. All members of the team are expected to be present. A 70 percent majority carries votes. A recording secretary will be appointed to be present at all meetings to record minutes, and will also be responsible for publishing agendas, minutes, and team memos.

Responsibilities

The focus of A.R.C. will be school-wide educational issues that affect student learning, such as staff development, supplemental programs and funding, discipline, school climate, and student assessment. The following areas will be restricted from consideration:

- Systemwide issues
- Personal or individual issues
- Issues at variance with established policies of local and state boards of education

Communication Teams

Communication teams will consist of certified and noncertified staff members and will include:

Administration Team

Classroom Teams

Support Team

Instructional Assistant Team

Staff Team

Each communication team will be led by a member of A.R.C. who will call meetings to disseminate information from A.R.C. meetings and gather input to take back to A.R.C. about communication team concerns. Communication team meetings must be held within 10 school days after A.R.C. meetings.

Task Forces

Task forces will be formed on the basis of school-wide concerns. Those interested in serving on the task force or presenting concerns regarding the issues will need to attend the initial meeting or notify the A.R.C. vice chairperson.

Each task force chairperson (not an A.R.C. member) will be responsible for making progress reports and recommendations in writing to A.R.C. A recorder will be selected to take minutes

Exhibit 3.4 (continued)

of each meeting. Minutes will be given to the chairperson of A.R.C. who will serve as liaison between A.R.C. and the task forces.

Standing Committees

Standing committees deal with ongoing concerns. These committees will include:

Student Advisory Team

Parent Advisory Team

Accelerated Reader

Discipline

Reading

Parent and Community Involvement

Media

Gifted Leadership Team

Hospitality

Gardens and Beautification

Decision-Making Procedures

The following procedures have been established for the decision-making process:

- Each A.R.C. member will have one vote.
- A.R.C. representatives may accept recommendations that are submitted on Issue Forms.
- A.R.C. reviews and accepts or rejects the recommendations by 70 percent majority.
- When a majority is not reached, representatives will return to their constituents for additional input and feedback.
- A.R.C. will meet a second time to reach a majority.
- If no majority is reached after the second meeting, a task force will be appointed to research or study the issue.
- The task force chairperson will submit findings to A.R.C. If no majority can be reached at this time, the issue will be tabled.
- Tabled issues may be resubmitted.

    Concerns submitted to A.R.C. that are not within the parameters of shared governance or school-wide issues will be referred to the appropriate group or individual.

Exhibit 3.4 (continued)

The principal, a standing member of A.R.C., will be present at all meetings and discussions, and will therefore be given the opportunity to disseminate pertinent information relating to issues. When a final vote is made, the principal will have one vote, as does each A.R.C. member. If the principal receives pertinent information that will affect a decision that has already been made, then this information will be shared with A.R.C. At that time, the chairperson can call for reconsideration and a new vote.

Amendment Procedures

Amendments to the charter will be submitted to A.R.C. A task force will be formed to research, write, and publish the amendment. Amendments to the charter must be passed by an 80 percent school-wide vote.

Decision-Making Rules

Charters include guidelines about how decisions are actually made, including a voting rule. The absence of veto power is frequently indicated. There is a great deal of variation among schools on voting rules ranging from a simple majority to two-thirds to 80 percent for approval. A voting rule may even exclude voting. Many schools consider consensus more appropriate and thus state that issues are not voted upon.

No matter the voting rule, it is critical to the process that everyone understands that a positive vote or consensus doesn't mean that some have not dissented at some point in the process. The charter should include the concept that once a decision is approved or adopted, everyone implements it regardless of their previous position. Shared governance is a process through which everyone is heard, but—as in Exhibit 3.5—no one individual can stop the school from taking action—the good of the whole is put before the desires of the individual. Shared governance must be understood as democracy in action.

When dissension is particularly strong, action research can provide information to help clarify the discussion and influence the ultimate decision. For instance, rather than considering full adoption of an instructional innovation, a pilot or field test to gather additional data may be warranted. This leaves a final vote open until data on the pilot project can be gathered and analyzed. It should be clear that if the resulting data is positive, those who initially dissented would more likely adopt the program.

Exhibit 3.5

CHARTER OF A LEAGUE MIDDLE SCHOOL

Definitions

Meetings will be on the second and fourth Tuesdays of each month, lasting for one hour. Emergency meetings may be called at the discretion of the Chair.

The agenda will consist of minutes, old business, and new business. New business agenda items will be approved by the membership at the beginning of each meeting. Agenda items will be submitted by the Friday preceding the next meeting. The agenda will be posted on the Monday preceding the next meeting. Emergency agenda items not on the posted agenda may be added by the Chairman with the approval of the membership.

A quorum will equal 2/3 of the membership. Decision making will be by consensus when at all possible. If consensus cannot be reached, a vote will be taken with the item passing if it receives 80 percent of the vote of those present (assuming a quorum is present).

Membership will consist of:

1 representative from each team to include the House chair and one each from the remaining grade levels in the house [Teams are organized into 'houses'].

3 representatives from the exploratory department.

2 representatives from special education.

1 counselor representative.

2 representatives from administration.

2 representatives from the support staff.

A year's term of office will begin on the first October meeting and last until the following September's second meeting. General Membership is elected to a two-year term. If attrition or team realignment creates a team with multiple or no representatives, that team will elect a new representative.

Elections

General membership elections will be held before the first October meeting with new members beginning their terms as stated previously.

Officer elections will be held the first meeting of October with new officers taking office the second October meeting.

Exhibit 3.5 (continued)

Officers

Chairperson

Elected to one-year term with two years in a row maximum. Must have been a member of the committee for at least one year. Duties: presides over meetings, appoints committees, calls and cancels meetings.

Vice-chair

Elected to one-year term. No prior membership required. Duties: fulfills Chair's duties in the absence of the Chair.

Recorder

Elected to one-year term. No prior membership required. Duties: meeting attendance, records minutes, prepares agenda, distributes minutes to all staff.

If the data, however, are negative or unclear, the issue should again be studied and brought up for further discussion and vote.

Subcommittees, Task Forces, and Liaison Groups

The School Improvement Team operates with the support of colleagues, students, and parents and is but one part of a larger governance structure. How a decision comes to the School Improvement Team and how the team functions after reviewing an issue are also considerations. Generally, the School Improvement Team can take action, delay action for further study, refer a problem to study by a task force, or refer the decision to the general faculty body.

The charter sets forth information on the role of standing committees, task forces, and other groups. In many League schools, liaison groups formed around a grade or team operate to ensure continual communication among and between themselves and the School Improvement Team. It is through these groups that ideas, suggestions, and actions are put before the School Improvement Team. Communication and feedback should be frequent. Liaison groups may also serve to gather information about a specific topic.

The School Improvement Team may appoint a special task force to work on specific issues, and such projects often require action research. Task forces have a specific purpose and a limited scope, and usually operate for a specified period of time before reporting to the School Improvement Team. For example, the adoption of a new reading series or other instructional sets may necessitate a task force. The use of task forces is another example of how shared governance enables both the covenant focus and action research efforts.

The School Improvement Team may also be charged with appointing standing committees. Standing committees operate indefinitely and oversee school activities in specific areas; an example might be the Library Committee or the Student Activities Committee. Standing committees frequently include members with specific expertise as well as members representing the learning community at large. Standing committees may be empowered to act independently of the School Improvement Team or they may report to it, depending upon need and the individual school. Regardless of the charge, standing committees like task forces operate within the focus of the covenant and function in ways that will bring the covenant to life. The charter in Exhibit 3.6 goes into greater detail on the subject of committees and task forces.

Defining Focus

Perhaps the most important component of the charter is to define the decisions that will be the focus of shared governance. It is not possible for School Improvement Teams to deal effectively with every decision in the school. As discussed earlier, League schools focus their energies on implementing the covenant, and therefore they make instructional and curricular issues the focus of shared governance.

Revision Process

Finally, a process for revision of the charter provides for orderly change. The final paragraph of most school charters describes the process for revising the charter. As in any organization, an orderly process for the consideration of new ideas facilitates change in a school. These provisions may include how and when changes to the charter can be considered. In our work we have found that beginning schools need to revisit and revise their charters as frequently as once a year. For more experienced schools, revision occurs less often and is frequently necessitated by a change in personnel, a significant shift in school population, or the addition of new constituent groups. Providing for change is a school determination and there is no recipe. As with the charter itself, the revision processes in each school are unique.

Exhibit 3.6

CHARTER OF A LEAGUE HIGH SCHOOL

Shared Decision Making Council By-Laws

Council

1. Composition: The Council will consist of 23 members. 10 will be elected by their constituent groups. With the exception of the members selected by the principal, terms of office will be for two (2) years.

2. Succession: A member may succeed herself or himself.

3. Vacancies: Vacancies will be filled by specific alternates if the alternates are still on staff at the occurrence of unexpired terms on the council; otherwise special elections will take place.

4. Representation:

   - Constituent groups (elected): One member from the following academic areas: English, science, math, social science, Magnet Coordinator, Program for Exceptional Children, a counselor, registrar, SST, and media specialist.

   - Two At-Large members (elected) from those academic areas not previously identified (foreign language, physical education, ROTC, art, vocational ed, music, challenge).

   - One member from the clerical and paraprofessionals (elected).

   - One member from the cafeteria staff (selected).

   - One member from the custodial staff (selected).

   - One member of the administrative staff (principal).

   - Two parents from the PTSA (selected). Those selected will represent the racial make-up of the school.

   - Four students (selected by student council). One from each grade level.

   - One business partner (selected by business partner liaison).

Council Officers

1. Co-Chairpersons (nonadministrative employees of APS): Set time agenda, preside over meetings, appoint committees, and call and cancel meetings. Present council progress and issues to faculty.

2. Recorder: Take minutes during council meeting, and prepare and distribute them to all constituent groups.

3. Time Keeper: Keep the council in line with timed agenda.

Exhibit 3.6 (continued)

Subcommittees

- Standing Committees: The types of committees and members of the committees will be determined by the Council. These will be ongoing committees.
- Task Forces: The types of task forces and the members of the task forces will be determined by the Council. Groups are to serve for a limited period of time.

Responsibilities of the Council

- Gather information and ideas from all staff.
- Establish priorities for school-wide improvements and organizing special task forces to address these issues.
- Make decisions and recommendations based on the work of the subcommittees and task forces.
- Collect and evaluate data needed to make school-wide improvements.
- Develop a shared decision-making plan listing measurable goals and objectives for the school year, develop a plan for achieving goals and objectives, and develop a method for evaluating achievement.
- Make all decisions in accordance with current board policy.

Elections

Elected members of the Council will be elected by their constituent groups in May. The person receiving the highest number of votes shall serve as the Council member. The person receiving the second highest votes will be the alternate.

Meetings

The Council will meet at least once a month on the third Thursday of the month and more often if necessary. The principal may select an administrative alternate to act as a representative at the Council meetings, but the alternate will not have a vote on Council matters.

Agenda

The agenda will consist of minutes, old business, and new business. New business items will be approved by the Council membership at the beginning of each meeting. Agenda items will be submitted to the Co-chairpersons by the Monday preceding the next meeting. The agenda will be posted on Wednesday before the next meeting. Emergency agenda

Exhibit 3.6 (continued)

items not on the posted agenda may be added by either chairperson with the approval of the membership.

Quorum

A quorum will be 2/3 of the membership. In standing committees and task forces, decision making will be by consensus, if at all possible. If consensus cannot be reached, a vote will be taken with the item passing if it receives a majority vote. No member of the Council will be able to veto its decisions. Once consensus has been reached in a standing committee or task force, the decision will become policy only when the Council has formally voted.

Amendments

Amendments to the By-Laws will be submitted to the Council in September, presented to the faculty and staff in October, and voted on by faculty and staff in November. For the first year, amendments will be presented and voted on as needed.

Procedures

Items not specified in the By-Laws will proceed according to the guidelines of Roberts Rules of Order.

Is the Charter Development Process a Long One?

Developing any charter is not always a smooth process and some schools may take a year or two before finalizing a charter that is acceptable to the full school community. Laurie Harling and Robin Sutton, early leaders in shared governance and League activities at an elementary school, wrote a case history of their school's development of shared governance from which the steps in Exhibit 3.7 have been excerpted. They refer to both the daunting nature of their task in working on the development of shared governance and the powerful sense of achievement in observing their school move to the application of democracy.

Developing any governance document may take time, but when the rules of shared decision making are written, everyone has a role, a voice, and a vote. As Robin and Laurie expressed it, "Making decisions through shared governance is an important step in creating change in a school. However, the true leap for a school is when each decision is weighed by

Exhibit 3.7

INSIGHTS FROM LAURIE AND ROBIN

These are the things that worked for our school. We

- Asked for outside assistance to better understand the shared governance process and how to develop the charter
- Developed an interview guide for interviewing staff by grade levels to get input about the needs of the school, the shared governance process, and how they wished to be represented
- Used data collected from interviews to define how the governing body would be set up
- Developed a clearly defined flow chart of the shared governance groups based on data gathered from interviews
- Drafted a charter outlining the roles and limitations of the Council
- Elected a group of staff members for charter review and revision
- Reviewed the draft charter in small groups facilitated by an elected review and revision team
- Presented draft to faculty
- Voted to field-test charter for one year
- Organized faculty into "families" or non–grade-level groups for representation and to provide a school-wide rather than grade-level perspective
- Sought nominations from representative groups and elected representatives
- Organized task forces as needed to study critical problem areas
- Set up a task force to review and revise the charter document at the end of the year
- Presented suggestions of draft review task force at the beginning of the following year
- Voted on finalized charter

Source: Harling and Sutton (1995).

what is best for students and the whole school. In this type of atmosphere, individuals examine each issue, research possible solutions, then select the best option based on the entire school's vision. Our school began shared governance six years ago. Yet it was not until a structure for decision making (our Charter) was created that we actually made the leap into true democracy."

What Are the Roles of Participants?

The role of all members of the school's learning community is to first be good participants in the process. Responsibilities include attending meetings of their representative groups, participating in discussions, assuming responsibility for action research, working toward consensus, and supporting and implementing decisions.

Team Members

School Improvement Team members have the responsibility of representing their liaison group or other constituency. Communication to and from the School Improvement Team and the liaison groups is the first responsibility of the School Improvement Team member. This is an important understanding. Members of the School Improvement Team serve to represent a group. Team members are expected to have good attendance and to actively participate at team meetings. The School Improvement Team members may also be asked to serve as representatives to an action research task force or a standing committee. Exhibit 3.8 provides additional details about team members' group participation.

School Improvement Team Chair

The person chosen to chair the School Improvement Team has special responsibilities. The charter details this role, the term of office, and selection procedures. The chair influences how well the team works and in what direction the team moves during the term of office. Both the chair and members of the team need the technical skills to build trust and support, to resolve conflicts, and to ensure that all groups are operational. The chair should also have the skills to facilitate meetings judiciously—to develop agendas, to keep people focused and on track, and to make sure all views are heard and recorded. For further suggestions about leading the group process, see Exhibit 3.9. Unless the team has designated otherwise, the chair is also responsible for communicating what has taken place at meetings by posting or distributing minutes, for conducting faculty meetings when decisions are brought to that group, and for ensuring that the succeeding chair receives all documents.

Principal

The role of the principal on the School Improvement Team is often the most difficult. It, too, requires a redefinition of leadership and the acquisition of new skills. As League school principal Jerry Locke says, "For a principal to serve on the School Improvement Team and to refrain from being the leader is expecting to see water run uphill. All of a principal's training and experience have helped to develop the role of a take-charge person who can make things happen. Yet, it is precisely the role of chief executive that the principal must abandon to sit at the table of the School Improvement Team" (Locke, 1995, p. 21).

The principal who is able to work as an equal and in a collaborative manner with teachers and staff on the School Improvement Team does not diminish his or her role. In fact, the role is deepened. Often this principal is seen as a facilitator-executive with commendable expertise who seeks to

---

Exhibit 3.8

SUGGESTIONS FOR GROUP PARTICIPANTS

1. Listen carefully to others.

2. Maintain an open mind.

3. Strive to understand the positions of those who disagree with you.

4. Help keep the discussion on track.

5. Speak your mind freely but don't monopolize the discussion.

6. Address your remarks to the group rather than the leader.

7. Communicate your needs to the leaders.

8. Value your own experience and opinions.

9. Engage in friendly disagreement.

10. Remember that humor and a pleasant manner can go far in helping you make your points.

Source: Adapted from Leighninger and Niedergang (1995).

help. Sergiovanni (1990) likens this role to other professions where senior staff assumes responsibility for training and mentoring junior staff, as with senior law partners or chief engineers.

Jerry Locke offers some advice to principals who are developing shared governance programs:

1. *Be a resource for the team.* Have a large view of the school and be willing to impart knowledge and expertise, when appropriate, but do not become the dominant player because of the information advantage inherent in the principalship.

2. *Listen, listen, listen.* On many occasions, the School Improvement Team will have to work its way through a problem step by step.

Exhibit 3.9

SUGGESTIONS FOR GROUP LEADERS

1. Set a friendly and relaxed atmosphere.

2. Have participants set ground rules.

3. Be an active listener.

4. Stay neutral.

5. Use open-ended questions.

6. Draw out quiet participants.

7. Allow for pauses and silences.

8. Do not permit the group to make you the expert or "answer person."

9. Let participants respond to one another's comments and questions.

10. Don't let the group get hung up on unprovable "facts" or assertions.

11. Don't let the aggressive, talkative person or faction dominate.

12. Keep the discussions on track.

13. Use conflict productively and don't allow participants to personalize their disagreements.

14. Synthesize or summarize the discussion occasionally.

15. Ask hard questions.

16. Don't worry about achieving consensus the first go-around.

17. Close the session by inviting group members to mention new ideas they gained in the discussion.

Source: Adapted from Leighninger and Niedergang (1995).

While it is tempting for the principal to "help" the team to an obvious solution, to do so would be to deprive the group of growth opportunities. And listening can be most insightful for the principal.

3. *Help find solutions.* Each member of the School Improvement Team has an obligation to help find solutions or ways for the school to improve. A major way the principal can help is to support the team in taking reasonable risks.

4. *Support team decisions.* Ideally decisions of the team would be unanimous or by consensus, but, if not, all members of the team—principal included—understand that they accept and support decisions.

5. *Refocus the team's efforts.* This is a nondirective, nonthreatening way to redirect the team's efforts and to provide gentle guidance in helping the team with its agenda, especially when the tendency to "go down many a side street" occurs.

6. *Watch the veto hazard.* In the concept of shared governance, there is no veto. Parameters should be clearly delineated in the charter to avoid conflict. Post a mental warning label that reads, "Caution: The principal's veto may be hazardous to shared governance."

7. *Borrow from the work of others.* Wonderfully innovative and effective models presently exist for school improvement. Replicate the many good and useful models already validated. No school is an island unto itself. Networking, affiliating, and reaching out are viable ways to learn from other schools that have previously set out on the journey of school improvement through shared decision making.

Central Office Personnel

The role of the central office is also important to the success of shared decision making in League schools. Most district administrations are supportive of school efforts in school improvement and appreciate the broad base of support gained in shared decision making. Districts can provide support by adopting policies that encourage school autonomy and supply needed resources and expertise. In some districts, however, the autonomy associated with shared governance is not supported. As part of a school's initial commitment to join the League, we ask that it secure the support of its board of education and district office. This step is essential to eliminate conflicts about the new role of the school. Communication and understanding are crucial in establishing a relationship of trust. Typically, the principal takes the primary role in communicating the concept, activities, goals, and outcomes of the School Improvement Team to the district office. The School Improvement Team should be careful to maintain its "locus of control," but should include personnel from the central office in its activities when appropriate, and should communicate its progress on a regular basis.

How Do We Tell How We're Doing?

Exhibit 3.10 on p. 64 provides a useful guideline for determining what has been accomplished and in planning what is left to be done. In the exhibit, schools just starting out will see themselves mainly in the "Emerging" column; those who have defined their work more thoroughly will be in the "Focusing" column; and those schools that understand the work and have implemented this aspect of the framework will be in the "Expanding" column.

In addition to using the self-monitoring guide, you may wish to ask the following questions. These questions can help shape the development of a school's shared governance process as well as serve as useful points of inquiry as the plan is used, revisited, and revised.

- What goes on in the name of shared governance?

- Who has been or will be involved?

- What issues are the focus of our shared governance?

- What role does shared governance play in relation to the covenant and action research?

- How do we know that shared governance is meeting our expectations?

- In creating by-laws that establish democratic ways of making decisions about instructional and curricular issues, what should we have included and what should we have avoided?

- What should we have included in these by-laws to promote improved educational experiences for students?

- What should we have left out of these by-laws because its inclusion detracts from our efforts in improving the educational experiences for students?

- How has the role of administrators, teachers, grade managers, or department chairs been affected by a democratic decision-making process? What have they stopped doing? What have they started doing?

Such questions help to ensure that actions and decisions are true to the intent of the charter.

Summary

Developing a program of shared governance and committing the plan in writing as a charter are not easy tasks. Schools experience a number of obstacles and impediments but find encouragement and help by networking with other schools which have had similar experiences. The school community will come to enjoy and appreciate its new role. Professional rewards far exceed the temporary disappointments experienced during the process. Finally, bear in mind that the expected outcome of developing shared governance and writing your plan in a charter is not to create a perfect document or process but to begin the development of democratic decision making in your school.

Exhibit 3.10

SELF-MONITORING GUIDE: SHARED GOVERNANCE

TRAIT	Component	LEVEL OF IMPLEMENTATION				
		1	2	3	4	5
		Emerging		Focusing		Expanding
Trait 1: Those serving in leadership positions are selected through a well-understood, democratic process.	Selection	Administrators appoint leaders after some consultation with stakeholders.		Some representatives are appointed; others are democratically chosen.		Representatives are democratically chosen.
	Representation	Only a few segments or groups within the school community are represented.		Representation is more inclusive, but limited representation remains.		All segments within the school community are represented.
	Voice	Decisions made by the governance body are regularly vetoed by one or more constituents.		Decisions made by the governance body are occasionally vetoed.		Decisions made by the governance body are not vetoed.
	Involvement	Only teachers and administrators are represented on the governance body.		All members within the school (for example, students, paraprofessionals) are represented on the governance body.		All members within the school and the school community are represented on the governance body.

Trait	Attribute			
Trait 2: Shared governance actions are aligned with the covenant of teaching and learning and informed by action research.	Focus	Decisions are seldom focused on teaching and learning issues.	Decisions are frequently focused on teaching and learning issues.	All decisions are focused on teaching and learning issues.
	Data Basis	Little or no data inform decisions.	Limited data are used to inform decisions.	Data are used to inform nearly all decisions.
Trait 3: There is an ongoing flow of accurate communication between those serving on leadership groups and their colleagues.	Frequency	Leadership groups rarely communicate with others, and communication is one-way and limited as to whom it is sent or given to.	Leadership groups often communicate with others, but communication continues to be between or among selective groups.	Leadership groups communicate frequently, engaging in two-way communication inclusive of the whole school community.
	Dissemination	Rarely are the actions taken by the governance body communicated systematically via minutes, newsletters, or other media to the full school community.	Actions taken by the governance body are communicated to the full school community erratically and unsystematically.	All actions taken by the governance body are communicated in a systematic, methodical manner to the full school community.

Source: *Demonstration of Practice Initiative (1997–98).*

Chapter Four

Using Action Research to Monitor Progress

At the base of the League's framework is the covenant, a collective vision of teaching and learning. Shared governance, the second part of the framework, is the decision-making process that ensures that decisions about the vision and how to accomplish it are made by the right people in the most efficient and democratic way possible. The third part of the triangle is action research, which is the process that schools use to infuse their beliefs and actions with the best information available both from outside and, most important, from inside their school. Action research is used to decide how to organize limited time and resources to transform the covenant into reality. Action research, therefore, is the collection and use of information for the purpose of improving teaching and learning.

The focus of action research may be any and all elements of the work that translates a school's covenant into action. This work includes student learning, instructional practices, curricular programs, staff development, expenditure of instructional resources, faculty selection and assignment, and instructional schedules. Ideally, all these elements are designed and aligned with the school's stated beliefs about teaching and learning.

Generally, action research follows a multiphase cycle of inquiry (Calhoun, 1994; Glickman, 1993). The cycle includes three basic components: identifying a focus or problem, collecting and analyzing related data, and taking appropriate action. The cycle is not linear; the phases overlap and a school will visit and revisit them as it moves through the process (see Exhibit 4.1). Action research is distinguished from other forms of research and evaluation by its focus on school-generated questions and issues and by its requirement of action before the research cycle can be considered complete.

Exhibit 4.1

PHASES OF ACTION RESEARCH

1. What do we study? _____

   _____

   _____

   _____

   _____

2. What do we collect? How? And How often? _____

   _____

   _____

   _____

   _____

3. How do we organize these data for sharing? _____

   _____

   _____

   _____

   _____

4. What do the data tell us? _____

   _____

   _____

   _____

   _____

5. What action do we take? _____

   _____

   _____

   _____

   _____

In League schools the action research process is tied to a school-wide plan to realize the school's covenant. It has widespread involvement of all stakeholders and an explicit timeline, and it uses multiple methods of data collection. There is someone responsible for overseeing the process and making sure that it is part of an ongoing cycle of decision making and action taking—plan, do, study (Demonstration of Practice Initiative, 1997–98).

What Is Action Research Used for?

When schools first begin action research, it may be difficult to see how such a process can contribute to the effectiveness of the faculty as a whole. In actuality, action research builds ownership. When action research is conducted for purposes exclusive to a given school, the degree and level of ownership of both the problems and the solutions increase among school personnel. People are answering their own questions about their students, their practices, and their programs. The personal and professional investments are high and the results can be powerful.

The experience of one League school provides a stunning example of the power of action research. This elementary school had a long-standing practice of retaining students who did not meet grade-level standards. The practice came up for discussion and examination, and the governance team of the school undertook a multiphase study of retention. First, they examined the retention policies of other schools and discovered that their retention practices were not in alignment with others. Their response to these results was that their students were unique and their practices met their needs. The outside evidence was not powerful enough to persuade them to change their practice. The team then examined retention research conducted by others. In this case, the research results concluded that retention was not academically beneficial, in other words, students who were retained did not "catch up" through experiencing the same curriculum and instruction for a second year. Again, the evidence was not compelling enough to convince the school governance team that their retention practice was not appropriate for their students. In the third phase of their research, the team studied their own students. They examined the subsequent academic performance of students from their school who were retained. Their study revealed that the academic achievement of their retained students did not improve—indeed, in many cases, students performed more poorly after retention than before. When confronted with these results about their own practice, their own setting, and their own students, they were convinced and they changed their practice.

We all act on a set of beliefs that we consider to be accurate, and it is only when we confront data that convince us otherwise that we change our beliefs and our actions. In this case, the school governance team believed they were acting in the best academic interests of their students. They believed retention was academically beneficial for students. They needed to study their actions and test their beliefs. On the basis of its own research, the school developed new guidelines for retention as well as new interventions for students who were not successful.

League schools use action research to gather information for several purposes. The chief uses are to gain understanding, to monitor action and progress on student learning, and to evaluate programs and practices.

To Gain Understanding

What is happening here? What do we know? What do others know? What actions have others taken? What actions might we take? All are questions school practitioners ask throughout the action research process. The school action research team seeks answers to such questions.

An example of this type of inquiry comes from a League high school. Growing out of a nagging sense of a gap between its current instructional practices and its staff's beliefs about good teaching, learning, and assessment, the school undertook a year-long action research study. Through surveys, classroom observations, student shadowing, and interviews, a task force studied the school's instructional practices and documented that the primary method of instruction in the school was teacher-led lecture. When probing for the reasons for this practice, the task force discovered numerous factors, including lack of knowledge of and experience with other instructional practices and lack of time within the standard fifty-minute class period, that discouraged faculty from engaging in more student-centered instruction. After examining and determining their own current practices, they started exploring what others had done when confronted with similar practices and issues. Through the League, they requested articles from research and practitioner journals, they attended conference sessions on related topics, and they talked with professors at The University of Georgia and other practitioners who shared their interests and concerns.

On the basis of the information the task force gathered, both from within the school and from without, the school developed a plan to put in place instructional practices that would reflect the staff's beliefs about teaching, learning, and assessment. The task force designed staff development to provide faculty with the tools, techniques, and knowledge to carry out student-centered instruction. It developed a scheduling scheme to provide for extended class time. And it instituted an action research plan to monitor the efforts.

To Monitor Actions and Progress

League schools conduct action research to monitor their actions and progress by asking such questions as How are we doing? and How can it be improved?

At one elementary school, writing was identified as an area for improvement for the entire school. Through a task force, a plan was developed to improve both the developmental stages of writing and the levels of skills. Staff development was designed and delivered and materials were purchased. Each grade level developed a grade-specific plan based on student performances and in keeping with the school-wide writing improvement plan. In the fifth grade, for example, the teachers devoted joint planning time each week to the discussion of writing strategies and writing instruction. Using data from their students' writing assessments, they selected writing skills or tools to focus on during the coming week and discussed how they might teach these skills or strategies. The following week, they shared both their teaching experiences—what went well and what didn't—and the progress of their students. Were skills improving? Was writing developing? They used this cycle to monitor and improve their instruction and their students' performance throughout the school year.

To Evaluate Programs and Practices

What happened? What can we learn from it? What should stay the same and what should be changed? These are evaluative questions that can be answered through action research.

At another League school, parental involvement has been a long-standing goal. Over several years the school put in place numerous outreach activities including newsletters, broadcasts on a local cable television station, multiple parent-teacher conferences, open house sessions, weekly classroom reports, and meetings of the parent-teacher organization. The school evaluated its efforts annually through a teacher survey by which teachers judge the involvement of their students' parents. According to this evaluation, the extent and level of involvement increased, and, therefore, the school continued these activities. After two years of improvement, the school experienced two years of no growth. These results initially produced great frustration across the school, but after discussion and reflection, the lack of growth in parental participation inspired a reexamination of the school's approaches to parental involvement. The school faculty concluded that they needed to take steps to better understand the barriers to involvement that parents experienced and to stretch their thinking regarding strategies for and purposes of parental involvement. They are currently developing an action research plan to gather additional information. They will interview a small number of noninvolved parents to determine reasons for their noninvolvement and will gather the results of similar research conducted by others. On the basis of this additional information, they will revise and refine their parental involvement efforts.

A second example of evaluative action research comes from a League high school's efforts to review its homework policy and practice. The impetus for this study was the faculty's growing frustration with the low level of homework completion. The team surveyed all teachers and administered a questionnaire to a random sample of students and parents. The results of the research yielded valuable information regarding the multiple aspects of the homework issue and suggested action that the school might take. For example, the data suggested that there was limited parental support and interest in homework, that students were spending very little time outside school doing homework, and that students, parents, and teachers often questioned the quality of homework assignments. These results helped the school evaluate the current use of homework and guided it in efforts to change the practice.

What Have We Learned About Action Research?

As outlined in the framework, action research in the League is tied to a school-wide plan for instructional improvement. It is specifically focused on teaching and learning and is a part of the school's day-to-day operation. League schools vary, of course, in their implementation. In some schools, we find loose associations between action research and school-wide goals, as in the cases of schools that are examining annual standardized test scores to measure their progress in student achievement. We may also find individual teachers conducting action research specific to their classrooms and interests.

The focus on teaching and learning can be elusive and, in some instances, intimidating. It is indeed difficult to focus on instruction. School management issues such as lunchroom operation, schedules for buses, special classes, planning times, or dress codes are the focus of some schools' research efforts. For others, climate, discipline, and attendance are topics of study. This is not to say that these issues are not important and are not legitimate areas for research. They are important and are often the subject of a school's initial attempts in action research. It is, however, important to distinguish between this type of action research and research on teaching and learning issues. Only when a study climate leads to an examination of the instructional program and practices of a school is it truly focused on instructional improvement.

The strong traditions of isolation found in most schools affect action research just as strongly as they affect the other parts of the framework. League premises require schools to break the isolation of individual classrooms or grade levels or content areas to focus on school-wide issues and concerns. The difficulty of that shift in focus is intense when schools conduct research on their instruction. When attention is turned to what teachers are and are not doing in their teaching practice, action research can reveal the tensions and struggles between the traditions of teacher autonomy—noninterference, lack of scrutiny, exercise of personal preference—and the shared responsibility and shared action of joint work (Little, 1990). In a League elementary school, the faculty adopted a set of language arts recommendations made by a task force composed of teachers from across the school. These recommendations emerged from an examination of individual and collective student achievement data and the district and state curriculum requirements. Among the recommendations was a need to emphasize vocabulary development, and examples of strategies were provided for each grade level. The action research developed to evaluate student progress in vocabulary used only student achievement as a measure. There were no structures put in place to support and encourage teachers to learn and implement the suggested strategies and there were no measures to monitor, guide, or evaluate the use or effectiveness of the recommended instructional strategies. When asked about these missing elements, one teacher responded that the faculty was not yet able to talk about their teaching with one another. This action research effort uncovered the traditions of individual teacher autonomy within this school and a lack of attention to professional development. This finding is not unique to this elementary school, and it underscores the need to attend to the development of the adults in the school as a crucial part of successful school improvement.

Although this chapter is devoted primarily to a discussion of action research planned and conducted by a school, external data can also be used to inform and guide the decisions of a school and help break the isolation of various members of the school community. This infusion of information from the outside can take many forms, including reading books, journal articles, and other professional literature, making visits to other schools, and attending conference sessions and workshops, staff development courses, and presentations by credible experts.

League schools have access to outside information through a League Information Retrieval System. Using this system, schools identify topics or issues of concern and interest and submit the topic to our office. We, in turn, conduct a search on behalf of the school for resources related to their request and send the school an information packet of relevant materials. A typical packet might include copies of research, practice-based journal articles, samples of materials, or Internet resources, as well as the names of university-based and school-based practitioners with similar interests, experiences, and expertise. The Information Retrieval System is one of the most widely used services provided to League members.

When planning, collecting, and analyzing their action research efforts, League schools can also depend on each other. League schools are an invaluable resource to each other. Each has developed and conducted its own action research and can provide suggestions and hints to schools doing likewise.

How Do We Begin?

As a first activity, a school might reflect on its current action research practice through responding to and discussing questions such as those given in Exhibit 4.2.

One point to bear in mind is that it is essential to ask the right questions—that is, the questions that will actually get the needed information. If we are not sure why data are collected, then their validity is questionable. Data collection must be limited and meaningful. We can't study everything or collect all the data available. We make excuses for negative data and often, if we don't like the implications, then we ignore the data and do what we want. It is hard to act on the data and not on our emotional reactions. And as difficult as good data collection and analysis are to achieve, they are the keys to the credibility and the success of both the process and outcomes of action research.

Examples of these action research struggles are found in the stories of many League schools. Data collection and analysis require skills and tools

Exhibit 4.2

BEGINNING ACTION RESEARCH ACTIVITY

- What information do we currently use to inform our instructional and curricular decisions?
- What data do we currently use?
- What are the strengths and weaknesses of our current use of information?
- What other data (available or needed) could we possibly use?
- What are the types of information that I find most helpful in assessing my own teaching?
- What information would help us set our instructional goals?
- What concerns should we have about the negative use of information?
- If we study a problem area and the data are negative, would we make this information public?
- Would the central office be supportive if we found we weren't making the hoped-for progress in some areas?
- Should we have a long-range plan for self-study?
- How much time and support would this take?
- Where are we going to find time to conduct this study?
- Will we be given support in learning how to do this?

Once a school or group of individuals has identified a particular topic or question for research, then the questions might become

- What do we know about our students as . . . (writers, mathematicians, readers, citizens, workers, scientists, artists, historians, problem solvers, and so on)?
- How do we know?
- What else do we need to know to design instruction and assessment, purchase materials, plan staff development, or organize the school day?
- What information would help us?
- How might we collect the information?
- What do the data tell us?
- How do we organize these data so that they can be shared?

that often must be learned and developed within a school. For example, when schools first begin to develop and use surveys, they often design them only to gauge popular opinion or attitude toward a topic or issue. And while what people think is valuable and highly appropriate to consider, schools have found themselves in the position of making important instructional decisions based solely on opinion. One middle school reported that it caught itself on the brink of abandoning one model of assistance for at-risk students for another based solely on a six-question opinion survey that was returned by only 30 percent of the faculty. This event led to a careful reconsideration of the school's action research practices and to improvement of its staff's action research knowledge and skills through additional development, better coordination, and the use of more outside assistance.

Other League schools report the dilemma of the survey du jour, a data collection technique that does not engender thoughtful response but rather devalues the importance of the process—wasting both effort and paper as surveys get tossed into File 13. For others the amount of data collected becomes an obstacle. A principal of a League school recounts the school's first action research effort. Using an open-ended survey, the School Improvement Team questioned every teacher and student in the school on a variety of topics. The surveys were collected and sorted into boxes—where they remain to this day. While the information may have been extremely valuable, the sheer amount of data collected was overwhelming—and therefore unused. The lesson that emerges from these experiences is that data collection efforts must be thoughtful, focused, coordinated, and limited. One key criterion for data collection—courtesy of the League of Professional Schools (1997)—should become a motto for action researchers:

> *The information we collect and analyze should help us understand and improve instructional processes so we get better results.*

How Do We Go About Collecting Data?

Use multiple kinds of data from different sources, across time. The chart in Exhibit 4.3 outlines some sources and types of useful data.

- *Existing Data:* This column lists the kinds of information regularly collected by schools. Motivated by their own interests as well as requirements of their district, state, or federal agencies, schools collect lots of information. These data are easily accessible and available and are the first place to look for information that might provide answers to your questions. The various items are mnemonics for a wide variety of actual data. For example, "Referrals" as a data source might include discipline referrals, or referrals to special or supplemental programs such as gifted programs, special education, or remedial education. It might also include referrals to guidance counselors, school social workers, nurses, or other support services. Likewise "Use of Resources" might include use of library media centers including both type and number of items checked out, use of technology and technology labs, use of equipment and supplies, or use of support staff. "Participation" could include participation in extracurricular activities, sports, after-school programs, free or reduced meals, clubs, academic assistance, staff development, and college courses. It should be a simple matter to develop similar ranges of data sources for the other items on the list.

- *School-Generated:* In this column are data sources developed for a specific purpose. They are obviously more labor intensive than those in the previous column when it comes to development and

---

Exhibit 4.3

DATA SOURCES

Existing	**School-Generated**	**Student-Generated**
Attendance	Survey	Work samples
Drop-outs	Interviews	Exhibits
Course progress and grades	Observations	Projects
Retentions	Shadowing	Portfolios
Referrals	Documents	Performance
Test scores		Displays
Use of resources		
Participation		

Source: *Hensley (1997).*

execution. These sources require the school either to develop the source or to adapt a source developed by some other group.

- *Student-Generated:* These are examples of student work that may be used as data sources. Again, these products may be generated for other purposes such as a course requirement but may also yield data that are valuable for action research.

The League recommends a number of action research strategies and tools that schools have found useful in the process:

- *Align action research with other requirements.* If your school is collecting information in preparation for accreditation or to comply with a district requirement, focus your action research on a related topic and use the data you collect for both purposes.

- *Organize for action research.* Many League schools use a form like the one in Exhibit 4.4 to plan and monitor their action research.

- *Provide leadership.* Someone or some group must give leadership to a school's action research efforts. In some League schools, a teacher or administrator oversees and coordinates action research. In a few instances it has been possible for teacher-coordinators to have an extra planning period to carry out their action research duties.

- *Offer staff development.* Arrange for staff development related to action research.

- *Get help.* The League schools that are the most successful in integrating action research into their school renewal process are the ones that got assistance from the outside (Allen and Calhoun, 1998). The ideal is to find someone who knows both the technical aspects of action research and the way it relates to school improvement.

- *Remember that issues are complex.* Keep in mind the complexity of the topic or issue you are examining and ask questions that reflect that complexity. For example, on a questionnaire you might ask a responder to list topics of interest or need for future staff development and follow that item with others that would ask for the responder to identify and describe the aspects of the topic that are of particular interest. It is one thing to know that classroom management is a topic of interest for a majority of faculty members, but it is much more valuable to know that one faculty member is interested in the management of experiential learning activities, another in management of cooperative learning groups, and yet

Exhibit 4.4

ACTION RESEARCH PLAN

Goal:

School Practice:

Data Sources	Person Responsible	Target Dates	Resources and Other Assistance	Results	Action

Source: *Adapted from Okey and Hensley (1992).*

another in management of transitions during the school day. Often broad terms need further explication to pinpoint exact problems or concerns.

- *Gather more than opinion.* Measure and consider popular opinion and level of satisfaction but do not let that be the sole basis of your decision making. Move beyond opinion. When schools begin to develop and use surveys, they often design questions that only gauge popular opinion or attitude toward a topic or issues. As discussed earlier, what people think about a matter is valuable and highly appropriate to consider, but it should not be the only source of data upon which you base an action or decision. If a school is beginning to implement new teaching strategies, it can be expected that initial levels of satisfaction might be quite high but would be followed by an often temporary dip in enthusiasm. This dip, known as an *implementation dip* (Fullan, 1991), can result in plummeting satisfaction ratings and can move a school to abandon a strategy prematurely.

- *Seek multiple views.* Look from different points of view, examine your question from multiple points of view, use multiple kinds of data, and collect data at a variety of times. All these strategies are a part of a technique called *triangulation* that helps ensure that you capture a truer picture of what is happening (Denzin, 1970; Mathison, 1988). For example, if you are interested in studying discipline infractions, you might analyze discipline referral slips for the specific types of referrals, interview a small number of students involved in discipline infractions, and conduct a survey of teachers regarding discipline referrals. To look at the same question at a variety of times, you could examine referrals over the course of a day, six weeks, quarter, semester, or year.

- *Be sure your data collection is feasible, doable, and useful.* Balance the need for multiple sources of data with the realities of doing action research within the busyness of school. Schools are awash in data that are collected but seldom examined and used. League schools often report that in their first research efforts they will ambitiously collect piles of data that no one has the time, energy, skills, or enthusiasm to analyze and report.

- *Use existing data.* Don't begin with the assumption that you must collect new data. Look to existing data first. What data have been collected that can help answer your question? Individual schools, school districts, and state and federal agencies all collect data regarding school action and performance. Standardized test scores, attendance data, graduation rates, participation levels in programs such as Title I, special education, extracurricular activities, after-school care, and postsecondary education statistics are some of the data typically collected and available for your use.

- *Use school and community resources.* Involve students and community members in your research. Integrate action research into the curriculum and have students design and conduct surveys and analyze and report data. Use students, parents, and other community members as data collectors. Students and others can conduct interviews, compile the results of questionnaires and surveys, and input data into spreadsheet programs.

How Do We Go About Analyzing Data?

Action research is a lot like popular journalism—you must ask the same basic questions about the data you've collected that a reporter asks when analyzing the information for a story: who, what, when, how, and where. Then it's a good idea to turn the questions on their heads and look at the converse—who is *not* participating, when is the phenomenon *not* occurring, and so on can provide dramatic insights into the situation.

It is important to keep in mind your research or evaluation question when analyzing and interpreting results. If you analyze and summarize your results as they relate to a particular question, you avoid getting mired in the data and losing sight of what you wanted to find out (Herman and Winters, 1992).

Data can be compared and contrasted in multiple ways. For example, you can compare data from different sources. How do classroom observations compare to the results of student surveys? How do students' performances on a unit project compare to their end-of-unit test scores? You can also compare results from one group with a similar one. How does the achievement of eighth-grade students this year compare to past eighth-grade groups? When comparing and contrasting data, you are always challenged to account for the similarities or differences. This type of analysis and interpretation can help identify or suggest possible and appropriate action to take.

Another way to analyze results is to look at data across time to reveal possible trends. This type of analysis is helpful when you want a long-term view of how you are doing. For example, you might track referrals for special education or attendance at PTO meetings across multiple grading periods to identify a rise or fall in occurrences. Looking at student achievement over a period of time can provide a more accurate and complete picture of performance than any single point can give you. Results from one year—particularly from one standardized test—can be misleading. However, if you track a set of achievement indicators over time, you will be in a better position to know if improvement is taking place or if changes need to be made. Limited or short-term results can lead a school to make hasty and ill-considered decisions.

It is often critical to disaggregate data to ensure that you understand how the phenomenon under study affects all the students in your school. Data are typically broken out according to various subgroups of your school population. Among the most common are race and ethnic background, sex, and socioeconomic factors. Depending on the question, it may be helpful to look at data in other ways as well—for example, by extracurricular participation, course or class enrollment, age, or grade level. Disaggregation of data can help you concentrate on what you might do to improve the opportunities, participation, or performance of all your students. In conjunction with disaggregating data, you may also compare and contrast data at different levels such as school, grade, course, or classroom levels. Often patterns will emerge at one level that may not appear at others.

How Do We Communicate Our Results?

It is often helpful to represent numerical data graphically or pictorially. For example, line graphs are helpful in revealing and illustrating trends in data over time such as enrollment numbers, incidence reports, or test results. Bar graphs are useful for comparing results such as standardized scores of different groups of students or test scores or grades across subject areas. Often, graph representations will reveal patterns obscured when examining only the numerical data. Many computer-based spreadsheet programs have graphing capabilities.

Also, narrative data such as journal entries, observations, or memos need to be organized and condensed into a coherent narrative. It is often helpful to organize the narrative around themes or patterns that emerge during the review. The data might also be organized around the various aspects or attributes of the issue you are studying. For example, in a study of cooperative learning, you might be interested in looking at the issue of accountability, in which case you could analyze and organize data around themes or aspects of accountability such as rewards and competition, grading, and individual and group accountability.

A caveat: at best, data can only partially represent something you are trying to observe and understand. Recall the earlier observation that schools are complex places, and that you can only capture a small part of what is happening in any given situation, relationship, interaction, or event.

The intended audience is a key factor in any decision about communications. It is essential to make sure that everyone with a stake in the outcome learns what they need to know about the process of action research and its results. At minimum, make sure the communications process takes into account the following points:

- *First and foremost, share the results with the people who gave you the information.* We've all completed many a survey or questionnaire that disappeared into a black hole, leaving us wondering what, if anything, resulted from our time and effort. That experience doesn't improve the reaction to the next survey to hit the in-box! Your respondents may not want to know everything you learned, but you should make every effort to share the results of the study they participated in. Sharing results might be an obvious step when community members or parents are involved, but it applies to students as well. Students are, after all, the primary stakeholders in the school.

- *Consider your audiences and purposes.* Research might be undertaken for multiple purposes and therefore might require a variety of formats for its reporting. A report to a board of education might look different from a report to a school-based task force. Likewise, what constitutes credible evidence often differs from audience to audience.

- *Make results of your research public.* It is critical to make public the results of your research within your school. This means sharing both positive and negative results. Finding out something is not working is often more powerful and useful than finding out that it is. To build collective ownership, everyone must have access to information and be a part of the decision making based on that information. The League schools that have been most successful in integrating action research into their school renewal efforts take steps to make certain that everyone is involved in the action research process as well as its outcomes (Allen and Calhoun, 1998).

- *Keep reports jargon free.* Almost every educator has met the parent, community member, or neighbor who wonders why teachers can't just "put it in plain English." There is absolutely no need to talk down to potential readers of reports, but the barrage of acronyms that accompany schools and school programs should, at the very least, be spelled out or explained. References to sources or terms well known to educators (for example, Piaget, Bloom, looping, criterion-referenced tests, raw scores) should be explained. The point is to keep the report clear, concise, and related to the points being made.

What Do We Do Next?

The key to action research is to remember that you never know it all. You can never know everything there is to know about a subject. The action research process is a *process* for that very reason. It is never finished. As you put in place actions based on your research, you are pondering questions that remain unresolved and raising new ones. You are collecting new and additional data to monitor and, perhaps, change the decisions you have made. The process breaks out into a number of more or less simultaneous steps:

- *Take action.* Even in the face of the humbling realization that you never know for sure, you must take action once you complete a piece of research. As Michael Fullan (1991) describes, schools oftentimes get caught in the cycle of always getting ready but never taking action.

- *Begin again.* Action research processes are not linear—they flow from one step or stage to another and back again. For example, you study information as you collect it, speculating on its meaning and drawing tentative conclusions, and then you gather more information. Likewise, when the action research is completed and reported, it is time to take action and to plan how you will continue to study that action.

- *Be prepared.* Action research will make you less tolerant of the status quo. It can lower the volume of dominating voices and give voice to those who may otherwise not speak. It will provide a way to make visible the invisible beliefs and practices within your school. It will help you examine beliefs and practices and provide direction for change. It requires trust, risk taking, and focus.

- *Track long-term progress.* Exhibit 4.5 provides a useful guideline for determining what has been accomplished and in planning what is left to be done. In the exhibit, schools just starting out will see themselves mainly in the "Emerging" column; those who have defined their work more thoroughly are in the "Focusing" column; and those schools that understand the work and have implemented this aspect of the framework are in the "Expanding" column.

In addition to using the self-monitoring guide, you may wish to ask the following questions not only once the action research plan is in place, but throughout the process. These questions can help shape the development of a school's action research efforts as well as serve as useful points of inquiry as the plan is revisited and revised.

- What do we want to know about?
- Where can we find the answers?
- Who is responsible for collecting the information?
- When will the data be collected?
- What is our timeline?
- What do the data tell us?
- How do we disseminate the information we have collected?
- What action do we take?
- How do we study the action we have taken?
- Do we need to change our plan?

Summary

Whether schools view their first efforts at action research as wading into the pool or diving in, such efforts are essential to the implementation of what the school community believes to be the best for its students. Without looking at where you have been or where you intend to go, there is no learning or progress. For the League's framework to work, all elements of the framework must be in place. Action research empowers the school community by providing answers to its deepest questions.

Exhibit 4.5

SELF-MONITORING GUIDE: ACTION RESEARCH

| | | LEVEL OF IMPLEMENTATION | | | | |
| | | 1 | 2 | 3 | 4 | 5 |
TRAIT	Component	Emerging		Focusing		Expanding
Trait 1: Action research is tied to the school-wide instructional plan based on the school's covenant of teaching and learning. Action research may be initiated by individuals, groups, the school community, or system or outside agencies.	Staff Development	Preliminary staff development regarding action research is conducted.		Loosely focused staff development continues through individual and group conversations, reading and reflection on relevant literature, conference and workshop attendance, and so on.		Action research staff development is part of a strategic plan that is focused and ongoing.
	Alignment	Individuals and groups are conducting action research that is loosely aligned with the instructional plan (derived from the covenant).		School-wide efforts are aligned with the instructional plan.		All action research efforts, of both individuals and groups, are tied to the instructional plan.
	Impact	There is little awareness of the impact of action research on the instructional plan.		There is a growing awareness among small groups and individuals of the impact of action research on the instructional plan.		There is full awareness among all groups and individuals of the impact of action research on the instructional plan.
Trait 2: The total school community is involved in action research.	Understanding	A limited number of people understand the existence and purposes of action research efforts.		People have a greater understanding of the existence and purposes of action research efforts.		The school community understands the existence and purposes of action research efforts.
	Involvement	Isolated individuals and groups or teachers are conducting action research.		Faculty and staff are participating in some way in action research efforts (for example, conducting, responding, analyzing, reflecting, consuming).		The total school community, which includes faculty, staff, parents, and students, is participating in action research.
	Collaboration	There is limited collaboration between and among isolated groups involved in action research.		There is increasing collaboration between and among groups and individuals involved in action research.		The total school community is implementing change based on collaborative action research efforts.

Trait	Category			
Trait 3: A fully developed action research plan is implemented.	Confidence	Staff are generally unclear and anxious about the action research process.	There is a growing knowledge and comfort level about the action research process.	A majority of staff are knowledgeable about and comfortable with the action research process.
	Format	The school's action research plan is loosely organized and incomplete.	The school's action research plan is written and tied to instructional objectives.	The school's action research plan is specific, clearly focused on instructional objectives.
	Timeline	Timeline is established but not necessarily followed.	Timeline is loosely followed.	Timeline is followed and updated as appropriate.
	Responsibility	Plan describes responsibilities for some action research efforts.	Plan describes responsibilities for most action research efforts.	Plan describes responsibilities for all action research efforts.
	Data Collection Methods and Sources	Data are limited to preexisting sources (for example, ITBS and other standardized data).	School-generated data sources are also included, and more than one method of data collection are used.	Multiple methods of data collection and sources are included.
	Analysis and Use	Data are collected but are not analyzed or used to enhance instruction.	Data are collected, analyzed, and used in a limited way to enhance instruction.	Data are collected, analyzed, and used to enhance instruction.
Trait 4: Results are widely known and are used to guide instructional decisions as well as to generate future research questions.	Analysis	Only data viewed as potentially favorable are analyzed.	Selected data are analyzed.	All data are analyzed.
	Dissemination	Results are disseminated only to those involved in the data collection.	Some but not all results are disseminated to school personnel.	All results are widely disseminated to the school community.
	Use	Results are reported, but no action is taken.	Results are used to determine action.	Results are used to determine action and to generate future research questions.

Source: *Demonstration of Practice Initiative (1997–98).*

Chapter Five

Applying the Lessons of Change

The League's three-part framework is a basis for lasting change. Implementing this philosophy does not constitute a one-time initiative or an add-on to what you and your school already do. The framework represents a process by which and in which school renewal can be sustained over the long run. The purpose of this chapter is to provide some thoughts on school change within the context of the framework and some strategies for making change an easier process. In conclusion, we discuss some of the ways the League supports the process, and some of the concrete results schools have reported.

What Elements Make for Lasting Change?

In an undated paper prepared for the U.S. Department of Education *(Changing Schools: Insights)*, Jane David identified several conditions associated with the real or "visible changes in what teachers and students do" (p. 3). She found that support from each other and the district; adequate time; individual and collective involvement; access to knowledge, skills, and ideas; and flexibility to make change all contribute to sustainable school improvement. These elements, as well as others, support the change process and are discussed more fully in the following pages.

Teachers must be active in the change process, as well as the principal and parents.

Like most organizations, schools will accommodate top-down recommendations (or even bottom-up) with as little substantive change as possible (Sarason, 1990). This minimalist adaptation generally leads to the failure of mandated change. For real change to occur, the ways decisions are made must themselves be changed. It makes common sense to have decisions made by those who will be most involved in implementing them.

Fullan (1991) captures the essence of the problem: "One of the great mistakes over the past 30 years has been the naive assumption that involving *some* teachers on curriculum committees or in program development would facilitate implementation because it would increase acceptance by *other* teachers. Of course, it was such an automatic assumption that people did not use the words 'some' and 'other.' It was just assumed that 'teachers' were involved because 'teachers' were on major committees or project teams. Well, they were not involved, as the vast majority of classroom teachers know" (p. 127). But real involvement, Fullan also points out, "makes people feel that they have a voice in matters that affect them, [so] they will take greater responsibility for what happens to the enterprise. The absence of such a process ensures that no one feels responsible, that blame will always be directed externally, that adversarialism will be a notable feature of school life" (p. 61). The greater the involvement of those who will enact the change, the greater the chance for success. Therefore, a shared governance process allowing for school-based decisions about teaching and learning will make for more effective change.

Change requires a realistic time frame to move from awareness to implementation and institutionalization.

Seeking the magic solution or silver bullet is understandable in light of political pressures faced by boards and educators and the limited funding and public criticism they must work with. But too many initiatives have failed in the pursuit of quick results. As David writes, "The greater the departure from current practice, the longer it takes for teachers and administrators to go through the stages from being aware of a new practice to knowing it well enough to appropriate and use it in new ways. It is about transforming the culture of an organization from one that is bureaucratic and isolates teachers to one that fosters and values collaboration, problem-solving, and continuous improvement" (in *Changing Schools: Insights,* no date, p. 4).

Even minimal changes will take time.

Educators need to be in touch with new ideas, effective practices, and the latest methodologies.

Implementing change requires that the school community think in new and different ways. Teachers and administrators need access to new concepts, the latest information, and opportunities to interact with other educators. We recommend that schools implementing the League's framework seek outside information, support, and resources. This may include interactions with other educators at conferences, active participation in professional organizations, membership in a network, acquiring the most up-to-date literature, participating in electronic discussions, identifying outside experts, or establishing a relationship with a critical friend. In the League, schools have access to the following services: a full-day visit to the school once a year by a practitioner colleague, a League staff member, or a university faculty member associated with the League; a biannual newsletter; meetings three times a year; phone consultations; two- or three-day summer institutes; and the Information Retrieval System. Schools use these resources to acquire the knowledge to implement the framework and to access the latest in current thought and practice.

Meetings provide opportunities to plan as a school team, to attend sessions conducted by other League practitioners, and to hear from national education leaders. The newsletter contains articles focused on the concerns of the schools and highlights the work of League schools. The Information Retrieval System, explained in Chapter Four, provides journal articles and other print materials about whatever initiatives or issues the school is interested in pursuing. Informed decisions are more likely to succeed. The on-site visit to the school is geared to find ways to assist the school in implementing the League's framework and to offer suggestions when and if needed. It is not evaluative in nature, just another way of providing information and assistance to the school. Some League schools find that one on-site visit isn't enough to meet their needs, in which case subsequent visits are conducted.

For teachers to change, they need new skills and access to knowledge and training, including research skills.

To change students, teachers must change (Maeroff, 1988). Most teachers and administrators have attended an assembly during the preplanning week before school, a session meant to pat participants on the back and charge them up for the new school year. Such gatherings are what Hall and Hord (1987) refer to as the "God Bless You" type of assemblies. Most have in common the pep talk, enthusiastically delivered, about the promises inherent in the coming year and the vital role of teachers and administrators in seeing those promises fulfilled, preferably before Christmas. Nothing is wrong with a good pep talk, but the general pattern of staff development as practiced in many systems does not have a direct impact on student achievement because it is unfocused; it's not connected to the needs of the teachers or the students or to the real work of the school. This kind of staff development ignores the complexity of teaching and learning—and also ignores what is known about learning and implementing complicated or elaborate new curricular programs or instructional strategies.

As noted in earlier chapters, staff development must be tied to the school's covenant. The kinds of staff development needed stem from the decisions made in implementing the covenant and arise from questions about what faculty and staff need to implement change.

Teachers need the technical knowledge to employ new teaching methodologies based on the needs of students (Wohlstetter and Mohrman, 1994) and to put into place curricular, instructional, or organizational changes. In *Changing Schools: Insights,* Elmore (no date) observed that a key constraint to educators acting on their beliefs "is limited access to knowledge on several levels" (p. 25). They need to know what skills and behaviors are necessary for both cognitive learning and problem solving. They need to know how to design learning, particularly across disciplines. Further, teachers need knowledge about curriculum development and what teaching should look like when geared toward independent learning (Wohlstetter and Mohrman, 1993). Without expertise, teachers can have little authority in the decisions they are to make (Maeroff, 1988). Putting in place governance and research processes also requires that teacher leaders and administrators know how groups work, how to assess anxiety levels, and how to reduce conflict. Such skills will allow faculty and staff to deal with problems immediately—an essential trait for success—and to build the capacity for coping with the exigencies of the change. Further, school staff need the opportunities and tools to think outside the box so as to make use of and rework existing resources. All efforts, however, will be driven by a clear vision of where the school is going and why the school community is undertaking a given change. Staff development should be planned around the covenant and based on data from action research.

This kind of practitioner-driven staff development ensures that needs are determined at the school level, that teachers engage in professional development activities individually and in groups, and that they are supported in assimilating new skills into their classrooms through such activities as peer coaching and critical friends groups.

Educators need real authority to make things happen and a support system for their well-being.

Nothing can demoralize a school community more than to see its efforts rejected. For instance, a League high school spent two years researching, planning, and developing a way to implement a new schedule. It presented the proposal to the board of education only to have it rejected. As a result of that rejection, the faculty and staff were thoroughly discouraged. The shared governance process no longer seemed worth the time or effort. Attempts to set forth substantive proposals for change failed; people didn't trust that they could follow through. The school lost its momentum.

In *Renewing American's Schools: A Guide to School-Based Action*, Glickman (1993) talks about the importance of having board approval in implementing the League's framework, site-based management, or any reform. Within the school the written by-laws cover how decisions are made and enacted (see Chapter Three). It is also wise to have any exemptions from district policy in writing. Beyond written exemptions, schools should double-check by clearing beforehand with appropriate district personnel before undertaking any effort that may go against the norm, particularly if the suggested plan will be different from those followed in other schools. Class scheduling and homework policies are examples where assurances may need to be secured before the school begins extensive effort in implementing different programs or policies.

To promote sustainable change, build a collaborative school culture where teachers don't just share decisions but actually work together.

At its simplest, "people need each other if they are to sustain change" (Joyce and Showers, 1995, p. 6). In another study on school reform commissioned by the U.S. Department of Education, researchers found that successful school-based reform efforts shared a set of core characteristics much like those found by David. In addition, these researchers found that establishing a school culture in which teachers work collaboratively is a necessary component of school success (Quellmalz, Shields, and Knapp, 1995, p. 3). If teachers aren't true colleagues, they can't learn from each other. Lawyers meet to discuss various strategies for clients; doctors consult with others to determine the best treatment protocols for patients; engineers plan with others for the best solution to a design problem; but teachers don't consult, plan, or meet with other teachers. Teachers are not accustomed to working collaboratively, or to viewing each other as true colleagues (Sagor, 1992). "Teachers, separated as they are in their classrooms, normally have little time to share and compare ideas. Professional growth is bound to be impaired in a setting where practitioners . . . do not see their colleagues practice their profession and hardly ever teach each other techniques" (Maeroff, 1988, p. 23). This isolation is the result of the way schools are currently structured and the way teachers are viewed from within and without schools. As teachers begin teaching in new ways as a result of actualizing their school's covenant, they need to observe and learn from one another.

Collaboration is equally important in the action research process because it builds a professional community by which to study and take action. It is the study of what is going on in the school that comes within the authority of the classroom teacher to act. It is data for the planning process. For Sagor (1992) it is particularly essential that teachers conduct their own research. As he puts it, "He who controls the data controls the agenda" (p. 5). For example, school reforms have often resulted from test data interpreted at the district or state levels resulting in top-down mandates. For schools to control their own agendas, they must gather, analyze, and interpret their own data. Eliminating or greatly reducing the control exercised by outsiders is essential to the success of schools. Teachers engaged in gathering information about their own schools and classrooms view their schools as learning labs to determine what happened and why (*Rethinking Professional Development*, 1996). They work together to bring about change. Sophie Sa of the Panasonic Foundation refers to the hallmark of a successful school as a "a professional staff that collaborates to make decisions . . . within a culture that encourages, even demands, questioning and reflection, rather than the mindless acceptance of tradition, convention, and habit" (Sa, no date, p. 28).

Change must be relevant.

Miles and Louis (1990) studied five high schools in five different areas of the United States and collected additional data through a survey of 178 large high schools. They found that for schools to change, the change must be meaningful and the faculty must be motivated to change. If a proposal is not meaningful, it is met with reluctance and cynicism. The value, here again, is for a faculty to initiate change through a process of study and a driving focus (the covenant). Which, or course, is implemented through shared decision making and then studied and revised as needed.

Don't change for the sake of change.

Action research data and the covenant define the school's focus. This prevents the proverbial quick fix approach to decision making. The instructional focus could be developing a new writing program, instituting a parent volunteer reading program, or implementing an action research initiative. Whatever the focus, it should be tied to the covenant and restated at all meetings, even listed at the top of the agenda. Without focus, meetings and conversations can come unglued and result in nothing but gripe sessions. Without a focus on what a school wants for its students, decisions aren't related to an ultimate goal. Activities such as those mentioned in previous chapters (see Chapter Two) keep meetings and people focused on what and why a change is being considered.

How Do We Build a Collegial School Community?

Acquire the necessary skills.

Accompanying the motivation fostered through site-based efforts, faculty and staff must have the skill to begin and sustain change. Although this has been mentioned already, it bears underscoring here for it's important in building the kind of relationships needed for the school to move together. People need skills to resolve conflict, to delegate tasks, to build relationships (Wohlstetter and Mohrman, 1993). It will take time to build the trust required to work through governance, instructional, and research issues. Focused, context-relevant staff development plays a key role here. Those who lead the shared governance council should be given opportunities to acquire group-processing skills and to learn how to conduct meetings and how to ensure that everyone is heard. Action research skills should also be part of what the staff should know in order to study the larger school issues. All in all, teachers, staff, and administrators in particular need the skills that will enable them to work more closely together—as well as skills that will help bring the covenant to life.

Check your anxiety levels often.

The way teachers feel and their concerns about the changes and challenges they are about to undertake should be of primary importance. Shared governance is a democratic process, which means that some teachers may have been uncertain about or opposed to a change that was voted in. It is doubly important, therefore, that people be kept informed, assured that the change will enhance rather than detract from what they presently do, reassured that they will be given time to adopt the change, and convinced that they are supported. Hall and Hord (1987) found that there are certain levels and stages that one goes through during a change process. Their Concerns-Based Adoption Model takes into account the perspective of the teachers in change and that it is possible to anticipate what will occur during the change process. Hall and Hord identified seven levels or *stages of concern* that participants will encounter: "These range from early 'self' type concerns, which are more teacher focused, to 'task' concerns, which address the logistics and scheduling arrangements with regard to the use of the innovation, and ultimately to 'impact' kinds of concerns, which deal more with increasing the effectiveness of the innovation" (p. 13). Self-type concerns are those one feels at the beginning of adoption of an innovation (for example, What is my role and how do I meet these new demands?) to full use and refining of the change (for example, How can I adapt this to better meet the needs of my students?).

Assessing the concerns of teachers and others is the first step in determining strategies to meet those concerns. For implementing the League's framework, the assessment of concerns may be assigned or undertaken by a task force or ad hoc committee of the shared governance body. Regardless of who takes on this task, it is vitally important for the success of any change that the concerns of those involved should be monitored and that interventions are implemented to address those concerns.

Open-ended questionnaires, surveys, one-legged conferences (informal hallway exchanges with colleagues), and interviews are some means of addressing concerns (Hall and Hord, 1987). Liaison group and task force meetings are two methods within the shared governance process that provide a mechanism for providing ideas to the School Improvement Team as well as for discussing concerns or clearing misconceptions.

As part of the process of building a collegial school, it is important to make sure that everyone feels safe in expressing an opinion. As a school moves to shared governance, care should be taken to ensure time for open discussion following the rules established in the charter. The full school community must have an opportunity to express concerns in an accepting atmosphere. Open discussions are a good way to determine where problems lie so that solutions can be sought.

Often people are anxious because they don't know what to do. Too many times teachers are asked to implement a new program or plan with little or no staff development. If teachers and staff don't know how to do what is being asked of them, then fear and worry turn enthusiasm into misgivings. Initial and continuing staff development is part and parcel of implementing the League's framework. When a school community understands from the beginning what shared governance entails or how to conduct action research or articulate beliefs and set goals, then the work will go more smoothly.

Redefine roles and attitudes.

Typically, principals have been seen as solitary decision makers, the primary authority within the school. Teachers have been seen as the technicians, the disbursers of skills and knowledge, autonomous within their own classrooms. Principals have also been viewed by teachers as their primary evaluator. In the not-too-distant past, teachers in Georgia were required to pass an assessment process for both initial certification and continuing employment. Under these circumstances, principals (as the primary evaluators) often made the only classroom visit a teacher received during the year. Thus some teachers may have a view of classroom visitation as being less instructive or informative than it is in collegial schools. Perhaps the new role of principal is more that of "head teacher," a role Glickman (1993) sees as harkening back to the days when principals worked alongside others in the schools rather than over them. With positive experience, the classroom visit comes to be seen as enriching rather than threatening.

The role of the principal as an instructional or administrative leader in League schools, however, is not abdicated. Principals continue to make the day-to-day decisions that keep a school moving. The governance process is primarily for teaching and learning issues, not for those administrative decisions that can be best made by the principal. The principal can provide useful information about organizational or policy issues or about state and federal requirements that may limit the scope of the governance process. This type of information defines early on what can be done and what can't.

The principal's support is, of course, essential. Without the willing support of the principal, only so much can be achieved. Chapter Three (on the shared governance process) offers what we hope is helpful advice to principals about this new role and how to successfully redefine their positions to fit a collegial workplace.

Nor have teacher-to-teacher interactions been seen as being colleague-to-colleague. "Teachers are relatively autonomous in their classrooms, and within a school they have surprisingly little to do with each other. They may identify with each other in terms of role and place of work, and they may have a feeling of loyalty to each other and the school, but it is rare that they feel part of a working group that discusses, plans, and helps make educational decisions" (Sarason, 1996, p. 141).

Building a culture in which everyone feels safe and trusts the intent of others takes time. It certainly involves more than faculty picnics, once-a-year retreats, or random bonding exercises. It is natural for teachers to feel uneasy when suddenly asked to engage in different decision-making processes, to conduct their own research, to state their beliefs, and to share their weaknesses and strengths with their colleagues. Joyce and Showers (1995) state that giving up isolation is probably the hardest thing to do.

"We find we liked autonomy. Thrashing out collective decisions is much more complicated at first. Studying teaching together is more aggravating than deciding how to teach one's own classes with one's best judgment unfettered" (p. 39). But in the long run all the effort is worth it.

Some teachers who read this may feel that with the loss of autonomy comes a loss of their individuality as a teacher. But the kind of collegiality we talk about is the collective effort of teachers to learn from each other, not an effort to rubber-stamp instruction. All teachers cannot teach alike, nor should they. It is in the classroom where that unique bond between students and teachers occurs and where teachers can be free to express their individuality in the way they teach and interact with students. Collegiality is about professionalism and what one can offer to and receive from colleagues to enhance one's own teaching and student learning.

But teachers and principals also need to look at students differently. If students are to have a say in their own education, in the governance of the school, and in how they demonstrate knowledge, teachers and principals need to look at students as responsible individuals capable of making correct choices. One League elementary school has a well-established student council where students police the playgrounds to determine what needs repairing, monitor halls, and make recommendations to the school's leadership council. One of the League high schools includes the president and vice-president of the student council as full voting members of the School Improvement Team. Such programs take time to build. Students also have to trust the faculty and staff. Beyond governance, students should be given more and more opportunities to plan their own learning, to develop their own projects, and to make connections to the larger community.

In the long run, "for the new order to be realized, every individual has to lose his or her secure place in the old scheme. Teachers can no longer argue solely for their own classrooms, grade levels, or departments. Principals can no longer resort to their status and authority in making decisions. . . . To make decisions in the interest of all students means to create disequilibrium" (Glickman, 1993, p. 91).

Don't be afraid to fail.

Unfortunately, schools are places where one *doesn't* fail (Senge, 1990), neither teachers nor students. Admitting not to know how to incorporate group work or technology into a lesson or how to mesh an English lesson to the social studies and art curricula is unheard of for most teachers. It is viewed as an embarrassing admission, at best, or, at worst, seen as a lack of competence by other teachers. But accountants or pharmacists or engineers don't know all they will need. Teachers should embrace the same love of learning that they want for their students.

Fortunately, schools are learning the value of pairing new teachers with more experienced teachers and setting up peer coaching, mentoring programs, and study groups. Teachers use these support systems to discuss problems, concerns, or new ideas with colleagues without fear of censure. In these schools teaching is recognized as complex and learning is continuous.

In a League elementary school, for example, the assistant principal started a group where teachers met voluntarily each week to share ideas and visit one another's classrooms to learn from each other and to improve their own teaching. The teachers reported that it produced some initial anxiety, but as their trust grew, the power of the collaboration emerged. They not only learned from their colleagues but gained a sense of worth and self-confidence in what they were doing. This group has now expanded to include most of the faculty.

Make time.

Time is one of the most limiting factors in implementing the League's framework or any major change envisioned by the school. The National Education Commission on Time and Learning reports that an enduring myth about time is "that schools can be transformed without giving teachers the time they need to retool themselves and reorganize their work" (1994, p. 8). The daily structure of how schools operate, however, limits what can be done about time. A League principal recounted that the single most important factor prohibiting schedule changes in her school was when the buses ran.

To find answers to this perplexing problem of time, a task force or ad hoc committee could research possibilities and seek solutions from other schools. Some League schools have received district permission to add minutes to their daily schedules by shaving minutes from lunch or other noninstructional activities to bank those minutes for released time one afternoon a month. Middle and high schools arrange schedules to ensure that department faculty have the same planning time. Some groups meet early in the morning or over lunch, or arrange for floating substitutes to take over classes and free up teachers for meeting time. Other schools have used parent volunteers to cover responsibilities such as cafeteria or bus duty to make time for teachers to meet.

Parents as well as school staff need time to meet. Although PTA meetings are an obvious mechanism, many secondary schools do not have an organized PTA, nor are all parents involved in the PTA. Therefore, involving parents and community members may require communication through channels such as newsletters, letters home, local cable access broadcasts, home visits, multilingual communications via newsletters or translators or e-mail. One League faculty met with parents at a local laundromat. If the communication is consistent, parents will be more inclined to read and respond to a notice about a school night set aside for discussion about the covenant or other issues.

Meetings for parents to get together and become involved in school activities will also require time from the faculty. Not all parents will be able to attend the same meeting, so alternatives should be made available—but faculty members should not be required to attend multiple sessions. Focus groups led by different teachers could meet over three nights to catch those parents who can't attend on a particular night. As a creative way to attract parents, a League middle school offered a computer as a door prize to attract parents to the school. Even though the computer was old and of not much use beyond word processing (and this was clearly stated on the flyer sent home) nearly two hundred parents came to the school. And another resource is for a business partner to donate door prizes or other incentives.

If parents are welcome in the school, they will more than likely participate in the work of the school. Several League elementary schools have parent centers, equipped with materials of interest to parents. Once signed in, parents are also free to visit classrooms—often escorted by their children. One school schedules a day where parents can attend school with their children, basically attending their classes, sitting at their desks, going through the lessons for the day, eating in the cafeteria, and participating in physical education, band, or art.

Accentuate the positive.

Sometimes negative thoughts about whether it's all worth it will creep in. Doubts sometimes lead to even stronger convictions. Work at keeping communications open. This goes back to an earlier injunction to keep everyone well informed, to provide frequent forums for the exchange of ideas and opinions, and to monitor anxiety levels. In addition to open communication, it helps to point out the successes achieved, even the small ones. Putting the League's framework in place with the goal of increasing student achievement will be done a premise at a time. Each process finalized, each covenant statement arrived at, and each student goal achieved should be a victory. Take time to note and celebrate each completed task and accomplishment. The same methods of communication can be used to note accomplishments.

Where Can We Turn for Help?

Networking

The greatest service the League provides its schools is the opportunity to network. Most non-League schools don't have a center that puts on three meetings a year where practitioners can meet with and learn from each other. But there are opportunities to work with buddy schools from within and across districts. Another school in your district may want to undertake the same work. Connect with that school for joint meetings. Teachers who have taught outside your school or district may contact their former school for such a possibility. The Internet has innumerable school sites where you can browse around to find a like-minded school and establish contact. And, of course, network at professional conferences.

There are also other networks like the League that provide a wealth of resources to their member schools. BreadLoaf, PACERS, the Coalition of Essential Schools, Comer Schools, Cornerstones, and the Southern Maine Partnership are but a few.

Facilitation

League schools receive a yearly visit from a practitioner in a League school, a member of the League staff, or an educator affiliated with the League. This on-site visit is to help schools implement the League's framework. On-site facilitators meet with faculty and staff, parents, and students to get an overall picture of the school's implementation of the framework. The facilitator is there to commend efforts, suggest resources or ways of meeting the needs of the school, and provide an outside look at the work of the school. Some League schools are setting up their own on-site facilitation through reciprocal visits with other schools or through an in-depth self-study of their own efforts.

A lesson we have learned—and we wish we had known years ago—is that internal facilitation is vitally important. A committee chair, special task force representative, or someone with a specific interest needs to be responsible for coordinating various efforts in the school. In Chapter Three, we talked about the importance of establishing task forces and liaison groups as mechanisms for generating ideas and for studying, developing, and implementing the results of those ideas. The chairs of these committees, for instance the action research committee chair, should serve long enough to see projects finalized and should have a certain expertise in what they are doing.

What Are the Real Results?

In the preceding chapters we have talked about the kind of effort involved in implementing the League's framework. Improved student achievement is the aim of this work. Current data include school case studies and observations, an independent evaluation, national surveys, individual research efforts of university colleagues, and several meta-analyses. These studies indicate increases in school climate and teacher morale, in staff development tied to the needs of the school, in student gains in individual schools, and in an increased focus on teaching and learning.

League staff, university colleagues, or practitioners from other League schools gather data from administrators, faculty, students, and others during the on-site visit to schools. Following the visit, the on-site facilitator sends the school and the League a summary of the visit. League staff apply certain rubrics to determine whether a school is a low, moderate, or high implementer. These assessments are used primarily to determine the level of assistance a school needs rather than as a way of "scoring" a school. These on-site reports, in addition to specific research conducted by the school or studies conducted on or about the League, are the League's primary data sources (Glickman, Allen, and Lunsford, 1994; Allen, Glickman, and Hensley, 1998).

Initial data about League schools from 1990 to 1993 revealed that schools focused primarily on shared governance. Since shared governance at that time was a fairly radical concept for schools and districts, faculties tended to put more effort into implementing this part of the framework (Allen, Glickman, and Hensley, 1998). The impact here was more on the teachers' feelings of greater involvement and enhanced professionalism. As schools became more comfortable with shared decision making, both they and the League began to place greater emphasis on action research and a focus on teaching and learning. Yet data on impact resulted from school self-reports and on-site observations, rather than from a formalized research effort.

Schools involved in action research did, however, report positive results from individual site-based efforts. For example, one elementary school targeted science as a main initiative as a result of data gathered and made this an instructional focus. "In just one year, the number of students scoring 80 percent or higher on a school science test went from 50 percent to 75 percent (Allen, Glickman, and Hensley, 1998, p. 17).

In the fall of 1994, League staff surveyed schools about changes in and across their third, fourth, and fifth years as members. Of all respondents,

97 percent reported at least moderate improvement "in student learning, participation in classroom and school-wide decision making, responsibility for implementing decisions, and attitudes toward learning (Allen, Glickman, and Hensley, 1998, p. 18).

During the same period, the League staff studied principals and the effect League involvement had on their professional lives (Glickman, Allen, and Lunsford, 1994). In a telephone interview of twenty-eight principals in second-or third-year schools, a trained interviewer who was not a member of the staff questioned principals about their role and how or if it had changed their relationships with the school community. Sixty-six percent indicated that they had moved from a directive to a facilitative, organizer role. Other self-descriptions included "encourager, supporter, organizer, and enabler" (Allen, Glickman, and Hensley, 1998, p. 21). Two of the principals, however, diverged from this. "These principals indicated a lack of trust in teachers' willingness to place the students' needs ahead of their own in making school-wide decisions" (p. 22).

In 1997, the League commissioned an independent evaluation of the work of League schools (Harkreader and Henry, 1997). Forty-five elementary schools that had been with the League for at least three years were compared to a general population group (all elementary schools in Georgia) and a self-selection group (schools participating in some other form of leadership program). These groups were matched to League schools by racial composition, percentage of students eligible for free or reduced-price lunch, and the socioeconomic status of the student body. On seven process indicators, the researchers found that League member schools had greater faculty participation than the other schools studied in both decision making and staff development activities.

According to the study, third- and fifth-grade scores on the reading and math portions of the Iowa Test of Basic Skills and the state's Curriculum Based Assessment were higher in League schools on ten of eighteen performance indicators when compared to the general population and sixteen of eighteen for the self-selection group. In social studies the achievement differential was significantly higher in League schools. The authors concluded that schools that implemented the League's framework were more successful for students than schools that did not.

In a report on the link between staff development and student achievement, Harkreader and Weathersby (1998) studied a sample of high- and low-achieving schools in Georgia across all strata and levels to compare the extent to which staff development varied between the two groups of schools. The authors found that among the higher-achieving schools, faculties collectively made decisions about their own staff development. From this research, the authors proposed five guidelines for effective staff development, three of which relate directly to the League's framework: employ collective decision making, focus on student learning, and focus on the classroom.

Even more formalized studies have already been planned. Since schools go through these rather lengthy processes each in its own way and manner, it is difficult to assess the League as a whole. However, as more schools implement the framework more fully and schools achieve comparable levels, studying the effects of League membership on student achievement will not only be easier but should reveal the extent of this work's impact on student success.

Summary

Implementing the kind of changes we have talked about may seem to some educators like trying to change a flat tire while the car is moving. But it has been noted that clearly focused shared decisions, redefined and collegial relationships, acquisition of necessary skills, allocation of sufficient time, and the collection and analysis of data are all components of successful change. Granted, it takes time, resources, skills, and commitment from within and without the school. When a school community decides to implement the League's framework, the people do so knowing that they are going to turn the traditional norms of their school upside down. They do it because to do otherwise would not result in lasting, sustainable change in their school, and therefore would have little substantive impact on the achievement of their students.

As you and your school contemplate the possibilities of the League's framework, consider forming a network, either formally or informally, with other schools. Share ideas and explore the resources included in this book and others. Given schools' track records for creativity in employing limited resources, we are sure that each school will make its own unique mark.

Many questions may arise during the process of putting the framework in place, and there will be dips in energy levels and enthusiasm; that's part of the process. We don't know all the answers, but we are learning with our schools as this work grows and evolves. Of greatest importance, however, is remaining focused on your students and their learning.

The mission of the League is to promote the school as a democratic learning community that is student-oriented and focused on improving teaching and learning for all. We would like to hear from you—teachers, students, parents, and community members—about the lessons you have learned in pursuing this mission. Each of you will add more knowledge to help other schools develop a climate and structure that enhances the lives of those in the school and improves educational outcomes for all students.

League of Professional Schools
124 Aderhold Hall
The University of Georgia
Athens, GA 30602
Phone: (706) 542–2516
Fax: (706) 542–2502
E-mail: lps@coe.uga.edu
Web site: www.coe.uga.edu/lps

Recommended Reading

Action Research and Assessment

Allen, L., & Calhoun, E. (1998). School-wide action research: Findings from six years of study. *Phi Delta Kappan, 79*(9), 706–710.

Anderson, G. L., Herr, K., & Nihlen, A. S. (1994). *Studying your own school: An educator's guide to qualitative practitioner research.* Thousand Oaks, CA: Corwin Press.

Bernhardt, V. L. (1994). *The school portfolio: A comprehensive framework for school improvement.* Larchmont, NY: Eye on Education.

Brubacher, J. W., Case, C. W., & Reagan, T. G. (1994). *Becoming a reflective educator: How to build a culture of inquiry in the schools.* Thousand Oaks, CA: Corwin Press.

Calhoun, E. F. (1994). *How to use action research in the self-renewing school.* Alexandria, VA: Association for Supervision and Curriculum Development.

Glanz, J. (1998). *Action research: An educational leader's guide to school improvement.* Norwood, MA: Christopher-Gordon.

Herman, J. L., & Winters, L. (1992). *Tracking your school's success: A guide to sensible evaluation.* Thousand Oaks, CA: Corwin Press.

Hubbard, R. S., & Power, B. M. (1993). *The art of classroom inquiry: A handbook for teacher-researchers.* Portsmouth, NH: Heinemann.

Sagor, R. (1992). *How to conduct collaborative action research.* Alexandria, VA: Association for Supervision and Curriculum Development.

Shared Governance and Collaboration

Bolman, L. G., & Deal, T. E. (1994). *Becoming a teacher leader: From isolation to collaboration.* Thousand Oaks, CA: Corwin Press.

Dietz, M. J. (Ed.). (1997). *School, family, and community: Techniques and models for successful collaboration.* Gaithersburg, MD: Aspen.

Kane, S., with Lind, L., Toldi, C., Fisk, S., & Berger, D. (1996). *Facilitator's guide to participatory decision-making.* Gabriola Island, BC: New Society.

Moller, G., & Katzenmeyer, M. (Eds.). (1996). *Every teacher as a leader: Realizing the potential of teacher leadership.* San Francisco: Jossey-Bass.

Saphier, J., Bigda-Peyton, T., & Pierson, G. (1989). *How to make decisions that stay made.* Alexandria, VA: Association for Supervision and Curriculum Development.

Democratic Education and School Reform

Allen, L., & Lunsford, B. (1995). *How to form networks for school renewal.* Alexandria, VA: Association for Supervision and Curriculum Development.

Glickman, C. D. (1989). Has Sam and Samantha's time come at last? *Educational Leadership, 46*(8), 4–9.

Glickman, C. D. (1991). Pretending not to know what we know. *Educational Leadership, 48*(8), 4–10.

Glickman, C. D. (1993). *Renewing America's schools: A guide for school-based action.* San Francisco: Jossey-Bass.

Glickman, C. D. (1998). *Revolutionizing America's schools.* San Francisco: Jossey-Bass.

Joyce, B., & Calhoun, E. (1996). *Learning experiences in school renewal: An exploration of five successful programs.* Eugene, OR: Clearinghouse on Educational Management.

Meier, D. (1995). *The power of their ideas: Lessons for America from a small school in Harlem.* Boston: Beacon Press.

Newmann, F. M., & Wehlage, G. G. (1995). *Successful school restructuring: A report to the public and educators by the Center on Organization and Restructuring of Schools.* Madison: University of Wisconsin.

Schmoker, M. (1996). *Results: The key to continuous school improvement.* Alexandria, VA: Association for Supervision and Curriculum Development.

The League of Professional Schools

Allen, L., & Glickman, C. D. (1992). School improvement: The elusive faces of shared governance. *NASSP Bulletin, 76*(542), 80–87.

Allen, L., & Glickman, C. D. (1998). Capturing the power of democracy for school renewal. In A. Hargreaves (Ed.), *International handbook of educational change* (pp. 505–528). Dordrecht, The Netherlands: Kluwer Academic Publishers.

Glickman, C. D. (1990). Pushing school reform to a new edge: The seven ironies of school empowerment. *Phi Delta Kappan, 72*(1), 68–75.

Lunsford, B. (1995). A League of our own. *Educational Leadership, 52*(7), 59–61.

Raudonis, L. (1997). The League of Professional Schools: Teachers and administrators working as a team for students. *Page One: Magazine of the Professional Association of Georgia Educators, 19*(1), 8–9, 26.

Rogers, D., Hensley, F., & Lunsford, B. (1997). The League of Professional Schools: Living democracy, building a learning community. *The Active Learner: A Foxfire Journal for Teachers, 2*(1), 29–31.

References

Allen, L., & Calhoun, E. (1998). School-wide action research: Findings from six years of study. *Phi Delta Kappan, 79*(9), 706–710.

Allen, L., Glickman, C. D., & Hensley, F. (1998, April). *Search for accountability: The League of Professional Schools.* Paper presented at the Annual Meeting of the American Educational Research Association, San Diego, CA.

Calhoun, E. (1994). *How to use action research in the self-renewing school.* Alexandria, VA: Association for Supervision and Curriculum Development.

Carlyle, T. (1965). *Conviction: The treasure chest.* New York: HarperCollins.

Conant, J. B. (1953). *Education and liberty: The role of the school in a modern democracy.* Cambridge, MA: Harvard University Press.

David, J. L. (no date). The process of school transformation. In *Changing schools: Insights* (pp. 2–10). Washington, DC: Office of Policy and Planning, U.S. Department of Education.

Demonstration of Practice Initiative. (1997–98). *Self-monitoring guides for implementing the League's framework.* Athens, GA: League of Professional Schools.

Denzin, N. K. (1970). *The research act: A theoretical introduction to sociological methods.* Hawthorne, NY: Aldine de Gruyter.

Elmore, R. F. (no date). America 2000 and U.S. education reform. In *Changing schools: Insights.* Washington, DC: Office of Policy and Planning, U.S. Department of Education.

Fullan, M. G. (1991). *The new meaning of educational change* (2nd ed.). New York: Teachers College Press.

Glickman, C. D. (1993). *Renewing America's schools: A guide for school-based action.* San Francisco: Jossey-Bass.

Glickman, C. D. (1998). *Revolutionizing America's schools.* San Francisco: Jossey-Bass.

Glickman, C. D., Allen, L., & Lunsford, B. F. (1994). Factors affecting school change. *Journal of Staff Development, 15*(3), 38–41.

Gutmann, A. (1987). *Democratic education.* Princeton, NJ: Princeton University Press.

Hall, G. E., & Hord, S. M. (1987). *Change in schools: Facilitating the process.* Albany: State University of New York Press.

Hanson, J. (1997, October). *Strategies for developing school improvement projects.* Valdosta State University and Okefenokee Regional Educational Service Agency, Eighteenth Annual Seminar, Waycross, GA.

Harkreader, S. A., & Henry, G. T. (1997, September). *A league of their own: Evaluating school reform efforts.* Paper submitted to Georgia Education Research Association, Distinguished Paper Competition.

Harkreader, S. A., & Weathersby, J. (1998, July). *Staff development and student achievement: Making the connection in Georgia schools.* Executive Summary. Council for School Performance, Georgia State University. [On-line] Available: http://arcweb.gsu.edu/csp/csp_staffdev.htm

Harling, L., & Sutton, R. (1995). *Our story.* Unpublished manuscript. Available from the League of Professional Schools, The University of Georgia, Athens, Georgia.

Hensley, F. (1997, December). Action research in League schools. Presentation at orientation and planning workshop, League of Professional Schools, Athens, GA.

Herman, J. L., & Winters, L. (1992). *Tracking your school's success: A guide to sensible evaluation.* Newbury Park, CA: Corwin Press.

Joyce, B., & Showers, B. (1995). *Student achievement through staff development: Fundamentals of school renewal* (2nd ed.). White Plains, NY: Longman.

League of Professional Schools. (1997). *Orientation and Planning Workbook* (rev. ed.). Athens, GA: author.

Leighninger, M., & Niedergang, M. (1995). *Education: How can schools and communities work together to meet the challenge? A guide for involving community members in public dialogue and problem solving.* Pomfret, CT: Study Circles Resource Center.

Little, J. W. (1990). The persistence of privacy: Autonomy and initiative in teachers' professional relations. *Teachers College Record, 91*(4), 509–536.

Locke, J. (1995). *The admiral dines alone.* Unpublished manuscript. Available from the League of Professional Schools, The University of Georgia, Athens, GA.

Maeroff, G. I. (1988). *The empowerment of teachers: Overcoming the crisis of confidence.* New York: Teachers College Press.

Mathison, S. (1988). Why triangulation? *Educational Researcher, 17,* 13–17.

Miles, M. B., & Louis, K. S. (1990). Mustering the will and skill for change. *Educational Leadership, 47*(8), 57–61.

National Education Commission on Time and Learning (1994, April). *Prisoners of time: Report of the National Education Commission on Time and Learning.* Washington, DC: U.S. Government Printing Office.

Newmann, F. M., & Wehlage, G. G. (1995). *Successful school restructuring: A report to the public and educators by the Center on Organization and Restructuring of Schools.* Madison: University of Wisconsin.

Okey, J., & Hensley, F. (1992, October). Conducting action research in schools. Workshop conducted at the League of Professional Schools Summer Institute on Action Research, Helen, GA.

Quellmalz, E., Shields, P. M., & Knapp, M. S. (1995). *School-based reform: Lessons from a national study: A guide for school reform teams.* [On-line]. Available: http://www.ed.gov/pubs/Reform

Rethinking professional development. (1996). Improving America's schools. Newsletter on Issues in School Reform. [On-line]. Available: http://www.ed.gov/pubs/1ASA/newsletters/profdev/pt.1.html

Sa, S. (no date). The need for systemic school-based school reform. In *Changing schools: Insights.* Washington, DC: Office of Policy and Planning, U.S. Department of Education.

Sagor, R. (1992). *How to conduct collaborative action research.* Alexandria, VA: Association for Supervision and Curriculum Development.

Sagor, R. (1996). *Local control and accountability: How to get it, keep it, and improve school performance.* Thousand Oaks, CA: Corwin Press.

Sarason, S. B. (1990). *The predictable failure of educational reform: Can we change course before it's too late?* San Francisco: Jossey-Bass.

Sarason, S. B. (1996). *Revisiting the culture of the school and the problem of change.* New York: Teachers College Press.

Schlechty, P. C. (1990). *Schools for the twenty-first century: Leadership imperatives for educational reform.* San Francisco: Jossey-Bass.

Schmoker, M. (1996). *Results: The key to continuous school improvement.* Alexandria, VA: Association for Supervision and Curriculum Development.

Senge, P. M. (1990). *The fifth discipline: The art and practice of the learning organization.* New York: Doubleday.

Sergiovanni, T. J. (1990). *Value-added leadership.* Orlando: Harcourt Brace.

Short, P. M., & Greer, J. T. (1997). *Leadership in empowered schools: Themes from innovative efforts.* Upper Saddle River, NJ: Merrill.

Wohlstetter, P., & Mohrman, S. A. (1993). *School-based management: Strategies for success.* Consortium for Policy Research in Education Finance Briefs. [On-line]. Available: http://www.ed.gov/pubs/CPRE/fb2sbm.html

Wohlstetter, P., & Mohrman, S. A. (1994). *School-based management: Promise and process.* Consortium for Policy Research in Education Finance Briefs. [On-line]. Available: http://www.ed.gov/pubs/CPRE/fb5sbm.html